Mrs. Morecraft's School of
Elocution & Composition Presents

The Young Ladies' Study Course for Proper Writing

Study Guide

Becky Morecraft

First Printing
Copyright © 2011 The Vision Forum, Inc.
All Rights Reserved

"Where there is no vision, the people perish."

The Vision Forum, Inc.
4719 Blanco Rd., San Antonio, Texas 78212
1-800-440-0022
www.visionforum.com

ISBN-10 1-934554-61-8
ISBN-13 978-1-934554-61-6

Cover Design by Kurtis Amundson and Ben Berkompas
Typography by Justin Turley

Printed in the United States of America

This study guide is dedicated to my daughter
Mercy Morecraft,
whose loving and patient assistance made the
production of my online writing classes possible.
Thank you, Mercy!

"Favor is deceitful and beauty is vain;
but a woman that feareth the Lord,
she shall be praised.
Give her the fruit of her hands;
and let her own works praise her in the gates."
Proverbs 31:31

OTHER CURRICULUM SETS *from* VISION FORUM

WWII: D-Day and the Providence of God

Into the Amazon Study Course

Biblical Economics: A Complete Study Course

Law & Government: An Introductory Study Course

The History of Christianity and Western Civilization

The History of the World Collection

Table of Contents

Introductory Remarks..9
Introduction of the Presenter 11
Acknowledgments..13
What You Can Expect from This Course................................17
Syllabus for Volume I..19
Syllabus for Volume II...23
Parameters & Suggested Tools 27

VOLUME I...**31**
Lesson 1–Foundational Principles for Christian Writers 33
Lesson 2–Laying a Firm Foundation: Good Grammar & Her Friends..........41
Lesson 3–Poetry: Harbinger of Hope & Glimmers of Glory................49
Lesson 4–Gathering & Planting 57
Lesson 5–Where Shall I Begin? A Few Novel Ideas for Story Starters..........67
Lesson 6–Journaling, Letter-Writing & E-mails: The Real You Showing Through......73
Lesson 7–Digging Deeper: Common Writing Errors 83
Lesson 8–Checking Your Tools—Packing Up to Go....................93

VOLUME II **99**

Introduction to Volume II Study Guide 101

Lesson 1–The Soup Course: Grammar Served Up with a Sprig of Parsley 103

Lesson 2–The Appetizer Course: Speaking & Writing with Agility & Grace 115

Lesson 3–The Salad Course: Tossing Together Clear Thinking with Clean Writing . . .123

Lesson 4–The Main Course: Writing a Sentence that Satisfies 135

Lesson 5–Making Miso Soup: The Clearness of the Sentence, cont'd 143

Lesson 6–The Dessert Course: Choosing the Right Word—Delicious Diction. . . 153

Lesson 7–A Happy Ending to a Good Meal: The Fruit, Cheese & Chocolates . 161

Volume I Answer Key 171
Volume II Answer Key 201

Appendix A: Poems, Quotations & Other Interesting Tid-bits 237
Appendix B: Sources and Resources 269
Appendix C: Pre-Writing & Story Ideas 275
Appendix D: Recommended Reading Lists & More. 281
Appendix E: Vocabulary Lists 301

Introductory Remarks

"Let our sons in their youth be as grown-up plants and our daughters as corner pillars fashioned as for a palace...." —Psalm 144:12, NASV

In the fall of 2010, Rebecca B. Morecraft began a series of classes under the general heading "Mrs. Morecraft's School of Elocution & Composition." These classes, originally delivered in webinar format (that is live, online instructional lectures accompanied with PowerPoint slide presentations) are intended to support more formal textbook instruction by encouraging anyone who desires improvement, particularly young ladies, in the areas of composition, public speaking and personal refinement.

Each boxed set will contain:

1. Recordings of the original lectures (15 discs which include each of the lectures and PowerPoint slide presentations)
2. Syllabi outlining "Volumes I & II"
3. A comprehensive workbook with study guides including:
   - Questions (with an answer key) for each session
   - Suggested assignments
   - Suggested writing exercises
   - Suggested resources for further research and study
   - Suggested reading lists
4. A certificate of course completion

Introduction of the Presenter

Rebecca B. Morecraft has been involved in the education of children and young adults for over 40 years as a pastor's wife, mother, grandmother and teacher, and is a popular author, singer and inspirational speaker for women's groups. Her treatment of the basic elements necessary for the development of beautiful personal expression in either written or spoken form possesses an "old world" charm. Her Southern heritage lends a gracefulness to her speech that enhances the extensive knowledge evident in the depth and breadth of her presentation of what could otherwise be dry factual information. She adds wit and charm to the presentation of layers of instructional materials, combined with caring personal involvement in her subject matter and audience. She delights her students as she informs them. This course strives towards the development of its students into mature, polished cornerstones who reflect their Creator's character in all they will be able to accomplish through Mrs. Morecraft's caring tutelage.

Acknowledgments

When I first mentioned the possibility of an online writing course to my friend Beall Phillips, I had something local in mind. I thought perhaps the Atlanta homeschool community would be interested in a few weeks of hearing me talk about writing. But when Beall mentioned it to her husband Doug, he instantly realized a greater potential. Thank you, Doug and Beall and Vision Forum staff, for encouraging and supporting us throughout the production of these online writing classes.

A heart-felt "thank you" to my respected friend Wesley Strackbein who took Doug's ideas for advertising our course and made it sing. You are such a good writer, Wes.

A round of applause for Michael Gobart and his customer support crew for helping with the scores of questions and related challenges that arose during the online course and with the production of these study guides. May the stars in your crown shine brilliantly.

Sincere gratitude goes to Susan Burns, Charlie Arehart, Joey Morecraft, Evan Nee, my "Welcome Spring" tea party ladies, the Boles, Bowman and McKeller girls and photographer Marissa Schmidt, and others who added layers of dimension to the entire process through construction of power-point presentations for the online classes, helping judge writing contests, technical assistance, proofing the study guide materials and much more. Thank you.

My heartfelt apologies and appreciation go to my family—my children, grandchildren, husband and extended family—that I have lived in absentia for the past two years, "so close and yet so far away," in Webinar-Land. I intend to make it up to you very soon, God blessing. Joe, how can I thank you adequately for encouraging me to exercise some of my "gifts and graces" in writing and producing these online writing classes and study guides? Thank you for patiently teaching me from the Scriptures and providing the Biblical foundations for my life. I don't know how to adequately show my appreciation to you, but I'm working on it!

And finally, thanks to my able assistant, my daughter Mercy Rebecca Frances Morecraft, who shines like a star in her father's house and in our hearts. Thank you for being there for us, always ready to serve our needs and those of others, cheerfully and from your heart "as to the Lord." Your encouragement, patience, acting abilities, photography and technical expertise greatly enhanced each class; but most of all, your willing heart encouraged and blessed me. Whatever was needed, you were ready and eager to do. Your invaluable help made this venture successful. From the depths of my heart, I thank you, precious girl.

In Alfred, Lord Tennyson's great poem "Ulysses," the speaker declares: "I am a part of all that I have met." I cannot take credit for knowledge imparted that I am now able to share through these classes. In my childhood, I was handed a silver chalice brimming with the love of beautiful words and stirring stories and I lapped it up eagerly. This addiction to reading and later to writing brings me great satisfaction. Its fruit has ripened and matured through the years. Now I pass the chalice on to others with the prayer that they will develop reading and writing skills beyond that of the teacher to God's glory and for their own enrichment. To those who pointed me in the right direction and helped hone my interest and abilities, I am humbly grateful.

I am grateful for each family who decided to listen to me talk for an hour or more each week about topics that are near and dear to me, due in large part to the loving tutelage of my parents and grandparents and many great teachers. Thank you, Mama, for reading to me as a child, often and with joy. Thank you, Grandpa Anderson, for passing on your love and appreciation of the Bible and great literature. Thank you sincerely, my dear Aunt Ginny, for teaching me to read when I was six years old. Thank you Mr. Burns Childress for making me learn how to write a concise sentence and diagram it in the eighth grade and to Jolene Hay for coaching me in dramatic reading and public speaking in the tenth, Negatha Powers for trying to teach me French, Dr. Peret and other fine teachers who red-marked my papers and kept sending them back to me until they were right. Thanks to Howard Deel who taught me to type in high school, to Jackie Sentell, Elizabeth Chapman and Dr. Loomis for voice lessons. Thanks to many others from whom I have gathered and gleaned knowledge and experiences that have enriched my life and love of learning.

I am grateful most of all, to my dear heavenly Father Who responded so generously to my request that He show me something I could do to advance His kingdom and encourage others from within the walls of my home. Thank you, Father, for this amazing answer to my prayer. I hope these study guides and recordings of our online classes will continue to be a blessing to many families and individuals who desire to strive for excellence in personal expression for years to come.

Soli Deo Gloria!
Rebecca B. Morecraft
Canton, GA
July 29, A.D. 2011

What You Can Expect from This Course

Although originally intended for young ladies, the usefulness of this course is not limited to the feminine sphere. Entire families have benefited from listening to these lectures. Mrs. Morecraft's desire is that, through both the instruction provided and her encouragement to excellence, her students will be inspired to hone their God-given gifts and graces, particularly in the various areas of personal expression.

The following syllabi for the combined lessons provide more specific information on the subject matter encountered in this coursework. Appendices include many of the poems, quotations, songs and anecdotes from the lectures, a vocabulary list drawn from the lectures with instructions for expansion of the student's vocabulary and word usage, recommended sources and resources for more in-depth study of the subject matter and recommended reading lists.

Use the study guide questions as you would driving directions which enable you to focus on reaching your writing goals, avoiding potholes and dead-ends, while enjoying a few scenic points of interest along the way.

As you begin this course, be sure you're buckled in—you are sure to enjoy the ride.

Syllabus for Volume I

Volume I introduces students to a Christian approach to reading various types of literature as well as an introduction to the expression of ideas through writing and speaking. The aim of the entire course is equipping participants to build a Biblical "grid" through which to sift, sort and understand various styles and genres of literature, as well as to employ their own gifts in these areas to the glory of God. Emphasis is made on learning to love that which is "true . . . honest . . . just . . . pure . . . lovely . . . [and] of good report." If there is "any virtue" or "any praise" found in a literary work, we will embrace what we can and leave the rest behind.

Some fundamentals of writing are introduced: grammar basics, writing styles, poetry pointers and story structure. Encouragement in various areas of personal expression and refinement is interjected throughout the series. Suggested assignments follow the study guide for each lecture. The Volume I lectures set the stage for those that follow by introducing students to topics which are covered more comprehensively in later lessons.

Lesson 1 — An Introduction to Personal Expression: Foundational Principles for the Christian Writer

Lesson 2 — Laying a Firm Foundation: Good Grammar and Her Friends—Note-Taking Tips, Verb Tenses, Vocabulary Building and Writing Ideas

Lesson 3 — Writing Poetry; Figures of Speech; Subject-Verb Agreement; Prepositions

Lesson 4 — An Exploration of Basic Punctuation and Good Writing Rules

Lesson 5 — Journaling for Fun and for History

Lesson 6 — Letter Writing

Lesson 7 — Developing Confidence in Reading and Speaking Aloud (by instruction and example)

Lesson 8 — An Introduction to Reading and Writing Poetry

Singing techniques, as well as using the voice expressively in acting, reading aloud and related topics, are introduced by example throughout these lectures.

Syllabus for Volume II

This second set of lectures uses metaphors from food preparation as a vehicle for a more in-depth study of selected topics from Volume II. These sessions emphasize the rules of English grammar, punctuation, guidelines for elocution (or how to speak and read aloud effectively), vocabulary building and an introduction to singing. Spiritual emphasis, appropriate humor and practical application are integral parts of each of these lectures.

Lesson 1 — The Soup Course
The Parts of Speech—Pronouns; Punctuation Rules–Commas; Conjunctions and Interjections; Vocabulary Building; Elocution Elements

Lesson 2 — The Appetizer Course
Speaking and Writing with Grace and Agility–Finding Strong Words; Subject-Verb Agreement; Punctuation Rules–the Semi-Colon, Colon, Dash and Period; Vocabulary Building; Elocution Elements

Lesson 3 — The Salad Course
How to State Your Thoughts Clearly; Punctuation Rules–Question and Exclamation Marks, Parentheses, Brackets and Quotation Marks; Subordinating and Coordinating Statements; Common Blunders in Writing; Elocution Elements

Lesson 4 — The Entrée
Arrangement of the Sentence Elements–Modifiers, Split Infinitives, Participles;

Avoiding Dangling Phrases; Punctuation Rules–Apostrophes; Agreement of Pronouns; Parallel Construction; Vocabulary Building; Elocution Elements

Lesson 5 — Miso Soup, for Palate Cleansing
Clarity of Writing Includes Knowing Which Words to Omit; Faulty Comparisons; Verbally Illogical Sentences; Punctuation Rules–Italics; Vocabulary Building; Elocution Elements

Lesson 6 — The Dessert Course
Choosing the Right Word—Delicious Diction; Dictionary Discussion; Conjunctions; Writing Dialogue–Use of Colloquialisms, Slang, Idiom and More; Verbally Illogical Sentences, cont'd; Etymology and Vocabulary Building; Elocution Elements

Lesson 7 — The Fruit, Cheese and Chocolates—A Happy Ending to a Good Meal
Review; Resource Materials; Vocabulary Building—Exploring Etymology; Word Choices and Common Writing Errors, cont'd; Elocution Elements

Parameters & Suggested Tools

Time Frame

Each lecture is 60 to 90 minutes in length.

Approach

My suggested approach in teaching the material is to listen to each lecture with the study guide in hand, stopping the recording from time to time to discuss the topics as they are covered. This would be a good time to answer the questions listed in the study guide for that segment or to emphasize desired points of interest. However, you may prefer to listen straight through each lecture and then go back and answer the questions. The writing exercises at the end of each lecture provide follow-up assignments.

Word Studies

The vocabulary lists found in Appendix E, provide assignments that will greatly improve your student's reading and writing vocabularies. Even familiar words will gain new layers of meaning if the avenues for learning connotations, etymologies and various uses of each word are explored as directed in the introduction section of this appendix.

Age Range

The targeted audience is very mature 12-year-olds and older. Younger children will be able to glean something from every lecture, but much of it will be too advanced for children.

Tools

1. A notebook with divided sections
2. A pen/pencil
3. A good dictionary and thesaurus (Webster's 1828 *An American Dictionary of the English Language* is highly recommended)
4. A Bible
5. Optional but recommended: a journal, beautiful stationery, calligraphy pens and practice sheets, a sketch pad
6. Although I will quote from many good resources, I only recommend one book as an additional resource for the serious writing student taking this course: *Writing to God's Glory: A Comprehensive Creative Writing Course from Crayon to Quill*, by Jill Bond. Although this is entirely optional, I highly recommend it.

Volume I

LESSON 1
Foundational Principles for Christian Writers

"To write you must learn quiet...If we cultivate the art of inner quiet and develop habits to nurture the mind's green fields, we will hear the melodies of Heaven."
—Suzanne U. Rhodes, *The Roar on the Other Side*, (a guide for student poets)

1. After listening to Mrs. Morecraft's introductory remarks, write one paragraph that explains why a Christian should learn to write and speak well.

_____
_____
_____
_____
_____

2. What famous ruler could not read but enjoyed being read to in the evenings? What was his favorite book?

Charlemagne
_The city of _____

3. Which English queen is said to have read at least six hours a day and was fluent in at least six languages?

Queen Elizabeth

4. Who penned this statement in a letter to her husband: "My bursting heart must find vent at my pen. . . ."?

Abigail Adams

5. Look up these writing terms.
A metaphor is:

Comparing something to something else

A simile is:

Comparing something to something else

[Note: we will cover figurative language more thoroughly later on.]

6. Ephesians 2:10 reads: "For we are His _____ created in Christ Jesus unto good works, which God hath before ordained that we should walk in them." What is the literal Greek translation of the word you placed in the blank?

Poem

7. Write a paragraph or two explaining the significance of the above verse to your life.

_____
_____
_____
_____

_____
_____
_____
_____

8. _____ is thinking on paper.

9. For the Christian, it is thinking God's thoughts after Him. "For as a man thinketh in his heart, _____." —Proverbs 23:7

10. Writing also helps clarify our _____. Writing helps us express our _____ and know ourselves and God.

11. "Without knowledge of _____ there is no knowledge of _____. . . . Without knowledge of _____ there is no knowledge of _____." Who said this?
_____

12. What are some good reasons to keep a journal?
_____
_____
_____

13. In story writing, as you develop characters and plot, have a definite point _____ and have a specific goal _____.

14. After choosing the general theme for your writing project, it's very important to choose which _____ you want to use to express your thoughts.

15. Whether you are writing fiction or reporting facts, it's important to make sure your writing doesn't condone _____.

16. "Nothing in life is as important as _____
_____." —RBM

17. Christians are the only ones who can see _how beautiful the world is_.

18. The scales have fallen off the Christian's eyes and we can see clearly the history of _____ and the hand of _____ in history.

19. "We must speak and write, through every imaginable avenue of expression – in _____, _____, _____, _____ _____, _____, _____, _____, _____, _____ – in every way that God opens to us, we MUST proclaim His grace and glory." —RBM

20. Essay question:
    "As a man thinketh in his heart, so is he." —Proverbs 23:7
    What does it mean to "think in your heart"? How does what you "think in your heart" affect the way you write?

21. Finish this sentence: A man lives like he lives because he _____ like he _____.

22. The Christian writes for the _____ of God and to _____, _____ and _____ others.

23. We live _____, before the face of God.

24. Convincing stories are powerful tools, whether they are __written__ or _____.

25. There are no _____ gray areas for the Christian.

26. Two proven resources for developing a more expressive writing style: _____ and _____.

27 You will get out of life _____ with the additional element of _____.

28. Great Christian composer J. S. Bach gave this good advice: "I was obliged to be _____. Whoever is equally _industrious_ will succeed equally well."

29. Multiple choice: The best way to discern the truth is by:
    ○ 1. My reason
    ● 2. The Word of God in the Bible
    ○ 3. What the majority of people say is right

30. What is the difference between the terms *denotation* and *connotation*? (Look them up.)

_____
_____
_____

Writing Exercises

Exercise 1

For this exercise, find a sketch or photograph of something familiar. During our webinar class, we used a photo of a little red-haired girl in a meadow beside a black lamb. (This should be on the PowerPoint slide for this part of the lesson). We'll use that image for this exercise, but you may choose to use another one if you prefer.

Make five columns on a piece of paper. The headings should be as follows:

First, list the naming words that tell what people or objects you see in the photo (girl, lamb, fence, sky, clouds, daisies, green, etc.). The column heading should be **nouns**.

Second, list visual or auditory images, descriptive words that your eyes or ears could see or hear (pretty, little, red-headed, dimpled, floating, spring, small, cuddly, laughing, etc.). The column heading should be **visual or auditory modifiers** which we will learn are either adjectives or adverbs.

Third, list sensory images or words that describe sensations of touch or smell (such as soft, wooly, scratchy, smelly, fresh, moist, dewy, splintery, etc.). The column heading should be **sensory modifiers**, also either adjectives or adverbs.

Fourth, list words that are descriptive of thoughts or feelings that could be experienced by the subjects in the photo, for instance: happy, thoughtful, joyful, frightened, scared, shy, relaxed, etc. The heading for this column should be **descriptive emotions**. These words are usually either adjectives or adverbs as well.

And fifth, list some possible actions the subjects in the picture could engage in to create a little storyline for the picture, such as: run, skip, gambol, feed, graze, rest, bleat, giggle, sigh, etc. The heading for this column is **verbs**.

Your assignment for this exercise continues as you write either (1.) a poem (rhymed or unrhymed) about the picture incorporating some of the words that came to mind as you looked at it, or (2.) write from one to three paragraphs about the picture using some of your descriptive, naming and action words. In order to make your poem or story more interesting, use a dictionary or thesaurus and look up the more common words. Find a word to use instead that provides more tangible, precise imagery, such as "ebony" instead of "black." Don't get too carried away with this! You still want to aim for "everyday" language with a slightly different slant that only you can give it with your particular word choices and phrasing. Read your poem or story to someone who will be honest and tell you if something needs improvement. Go back to your piece, edit and re-write it.

Exercise 2

Research the book *Writing to God's Glory: A Comprehensive Creative Writing Course from Crayon to Quill*, by Jill Bond. Begin following her instructions for the teacher, pages 1-136. Student activities and exercises begin on page 139. You may choose the pace at which you will cover this book, fitting it to your needs.

Exercise 3: Vocabulary and Word-Building

Go to the vocabulary pages in Appendix E. You will find words on these pages that I have extracted from my lectures. Please follow the instructions explaining how to utilize these lists in order to increase both your reading and your writing vocabulary. I suggest that you try to add at least 10 words at a time to your list until you have added all of them to your vocabulary list. Never mind that some of the words are very familiar—look up their various usages, etymologies and other related information. However, if you have already done this kind of thorough word study on a listed word and would like to choose another word from the dictionary page with which you are less familiar, please do so. You may be surprised how these exercises will strengthen your ability to use strong words effectively in your writing.

LESSON 2
Laying a Firm Foundation—Good Grammar & Her Friends

"...the trendy, the senseless, and the merely pretty fall dead on the battlefield, and only the truly valuable [writings] survive."
—Gary Provost, *100 Ways to Improve Your Writing*, p. 108.

1. Note-taking during a lecture, sermon or speech can be highly beneficial for memory retention. List a few suggestions for improving your note-taking skills.

   _____
   _____
   _____

2. Three large word groupings are _____, _____ and _____.

3. _____ is a description of both clear writing that isn't cluttered with too many modifiers as well as the best way to dress.

4. Be a word _____ and add interesting words to your vocabulary often.

5. A common grammatical error is made when we _____ _____ in the middle of a sentence.

6. List the basic verb tenses and give two examples in each category (there are three tenses and numerous forms that can be made from them).

_____
_____
_____
_____

7. The _____ tense of a verb expresses an unchanging, repeated or re-occurring action or a situation that exists only now. It can also represent an _____.

8. Draw a line from the sentence on the left to the correct meaning on the right to correctly match the present tense verbs in each sentence with their meaning.

   a. The ocean tides ebb and flow.   i. acknowledged fact
   b. Every winter, snow covers the pasture. ii. unchanging action
   c. Italy is located in Europe.   iii. recurring action

9. Past tense verbs express an action or situation that was _____ and _____ in the past.

10. Most past tense verbs end in _____, but some have special past tense forms called _____ verbs whose forms have to be memorized.

11. Choose a verb and correctly write at least three sentences using different verb tenses.

Example: to make
"I make my bed every morning." (present tense)
"I am making my bed right now." (present tense, progressive form)
"I will make my bed tomorrow." (future tense)
"I could make my bed in the evening, but I don't." (present tense, conditional)
"I made my bed 365 times last year." (past tense)
"I will have made my bed seven times this week by tomorrow morning." (future perfect tense)

_____
_____
_____
_____
_____
_____

12. The most important thing to remember is not to _____ verb tenses in a sentence.

13. True or false? Even though it's great to learn the proper rules for writing, sometimes the best writing is that which ignores the rules. _____

14. A short story is often called a _____ which is French for a decorative drawing small enough to draw or write on a leaf.

15. Another way to think of a short story of this kind is to imagine it as a tiny _____ taken with the _____ of the eyes and sent to the brain for _____.

16. List some considerations that will help you write a good story that are mentioned in connection with this part of the lecture.

_____
_____

_____

_____

_____

17. Although we can train our brains to learn the rules of good grammar and other writing techniques, there is a _____ involved in good writing that is hard to explain.

18. "All of life's _____—those you can call to mind, and many that are locked away in the dark recesses of some fold of your complex brain—will be brought to bear on what you write." —RBM

19. Practice reading the quoted lines from Alfred, Lord Tennyson's poem "Ulysses" aloud. Emphasize the important words and practice carrying the sentences through, pausing only at commas, colons or semi-colons, not at the end of lines. Try to find any existing internal rhyme, that is, words with similar vowel sounds or end rhymes that are not placed at the end of a line. (See Appendix A: Poems, Quotations and Other Interesting Tid-Bits to locate this part of the poem).

20. "To write, _____." —Suzanne Rhodes

21. List a few tips to help you prepare to write.

_____

_____

_____

_____

22. True of false? When you write a story that illustrates Biblical principles, whether you mention God or not, you are writing with a "sanctified" mindset.
_____

23. Graceful writing that is widely read and accepted should be based on _____.

24. Some good methods for developing writing skills are:

_____
_____
_____
_____

25. A good way to overcome "writer's block" is _____.

26. Always proof your writing and be your own worst critic. Robert Frost said, "A poem is never finished, it's only _____."

Writing Exercises

Exercise 1

Choose one of the following from which to gather words:
- Seed catalogs
- Magazine articles
- A favorite book
- A Bible
- A newspaper
- A songbook
- A cookbook
- Some other publication of your choice

Take a plain sheet of paper and make four columns with these headings: nouns, verbs, modifiers and phrases or quotations.

Flip through your printed material and extract the most interesting words and phrases from each category and list them in the proper column. After you've found approximately 10 words for each category, write one of the following: a short story, a three-paragraph essay, an article, a blog post, a poem, a song or an advertisement using some form of your gleaned words. Make sure to look up exact meanings so that you know both the *denotation* and *connotation* of the words and use them correctly.

Go back over your work and check for:

- Correct verb tenses that "match"
- Spelling
- Content that will keep your reader interested from the first sentence
- Ask yourself if you have accomplished your writing goal for the piece.
- Do the words flow together or does it sound too choppy?
- Are your verbs strong?
- Is each of the nouns the exact word you needed to express your thought?
- Did you convey the information or feelings you wanted to convey in the piece?
- Is your grammar correct?

Read it aloud to yourself and then to a friend and listen to his criticism. Go back and make any necessary changes and save your piece so that you can review it at the end of this course and see how much you've learned. If you really like it, send it to me at **mrs.morecraft@gmail.com**. Have fun!

Exercise 2

Think about the term "vignette" mentioned in this lecture. Try your hand at writing some tiny "word pictures," a one-three sentence little snapshot of something that you've seen, experienced, tasted, smelt, felt or wished or dreaded. Have fun!

Exercise 3

Continue with the next portion of *Writing to God's Glory* by Jill Bond.

Exercise 4: Vocabulary and Word-Building

Go to Appendix E and follow the suggestions for adding vocabulary words from this lecture to your list. I suggest adding 5-10 words a day until you've completed this section. Be sure to follow each instruction so that you will "own" the new word or make improvement on using words with which you may be already somewhat familiar.

LESSON 3
Poetry: Harbinger of Hope & Glimmers of Glory

"Prose is words in their best order; poetry is the best words in their best order."
—Samuel Taylor Coleridge

1. God created the universe and all it contains _____ _____, a Latin phrase meaning "out of nothing."

2. True or false: God created the world because He was lonely. _____

3. John 1:1 says that Jesus was there at the beginning of all things and identifies Him as _____.

4. Poetic language can be used to expand our thoughts beyond simple _____ sequences of words to express _____ _____.

5. Poetic language impels us to speak and think in more _____ _____, although not necessarily using more _____ words.

6. Elements of good poetry consist of: the conveyance of _____, the depiction of _____ and _____ that illicit deeper understanding on the part of the reader.

7. The _____ is replete with poetic imagery.

8. Give some examples of poetic imagery in the form of **metaphor** found in the Bible.

_____
_____

9. Give some examples of poetic imagery in the form of **simile** found in the Bible.

_____
_____

10. "Not only should our prose convey _____, _____ imagery, but we should learn to love to read and write poetry that is full of _____, _____ images." —RBM

11. William Wordsworth described poetry as "the spontaneous overflow of _____ _____," which takes its "origin from _____ recollected in tranquility."

12. Eudora Welty suggested four characteristics of good writing. What are they?

_____
_____
_____
_____

13. Define these terms which are used to designate types of figurative language: *personification, apostrophe, hyperbole, understatement, metaphor* and *simile* Give an example of each.

_____
_____
_____

14. Finish this sentence: "Because poetry is a language of intense feeling, figures of speech are fitted well to _____ the _____."

15. A technical phrase used to designate "figurative speech" is the phrase _____ _____.

16. Metaphors are used in _____ of the object or idea being described, while similes always use _____ or _____ to begin the comparison.

17. Jesus often used metaphors to refer to Himself in the Bible. How many can you name?

_____
_____

18. Go through a few chapters in the book of Proverbs and list some metaphors and similes you find there. Keep a list in your notebook of literary devices and figures of speech that you discover as you read your Bible or other sources.

_____
_____
_____
_____

19. Plural subjects require _____ verbs and singular subjects require _____ verbs.

20. One of the problems encountered in long, complex sentences is _____ – _____ agreement.

21. Write two sentences illustrating the point made above.

_____

_____

_____

_____

22. An easy way to remember the definition of a preposition is that the letters after "pre" spell "position." Prepositions often tell the position of something. List some prepositions below.

_____

_____

23. A _____ is a word that shows how a noun or pronoun relates to another part of the sentence.

24. As a rule, don't use prepositions when _____.

25. In formal writing, don't end a sentence with a _____.

26. However, in informal conversation, sometimes this rule can be broken if it is less _____. For example, which sentence sounds more natural: a.) "Who are you going to church with?" (ends in a preposition) or, b.) "With whom are you going to church?" _____

27. Go to "Top Ten Ideas to Help your Children Become Better Writers" from Carmon Friedrich's *Buried Treasure* blog at **buriedtreasurebooks.com** and extract some helpful ideas.

28. Listen to Doug Phillips read Alfred, Lord Tennyson's "The Charge of the Light Brigade," either from the lesson recording or from the audio version of *Poems for Patriarchs*, available from Vision Forum. Listen to the modulations of his voice that exactly match the emotion expressed by the poet. After listening to the poem, find it in Appendix A and read it aloud until you are satisfied that your reading matches his in voice quality, inflection, accent and tone.

29. "There are many legitimate reasons for writing poetry; but consider writing poetry that will turn heads, grasp attention, convict hearts and _____ ____ _____ of your generation." —RBM

30. What are suggestions offered by Mr. Moore who is quoted in the lecture for the serious, culture-changing poet to consider?

_____
_____
_____

Writing Exercises

(I want to thank my friend, poetess and teacher, Suzanne Rhodes, for many of the suggestions offered in these exercises and elsewhere.)

Exercise 1: Finding Your Own "Personal" Metaphor/Word Association

Pick one word or phrase to use as a metaphor, something that has significance to you, that fits your personality, your gifts, your inclinations, and your circumstances.

• A word or phrase like: spring-time, rain, baby, shadow, seed, green, shell, pebble, unfolding flower, blue, river, rock, or another word or phrase of your choosing.

- You may wish to use an image from Scripture, like lamp, branch, vine, temple, spring, well, sheep, pilgrim, pearl, farmer, athlete, field. . . you choose.

Here's what to do with it:

Allow this metaphor to paint a picture in your imagination. Let your senses enter into it and enlarge it. What feeling, emotion, taste, smell, appearance or sound does it evoke? Jot down all the words and ideas that this nucleus word brings to mind, clustering them around the nucleus word in a web, as diagrammed in the drawing from the slide-show from this lecture.

In other words, draw a circle containing a central word with arrows pointing to twenty or so associated words written in separate but sometimes connected circles.

1. Now, tie the best of these associated ideas together, building a brief poem, reflection, story or essay around this central metaphor, which emanates from you and your memory store. Keep your writing concrete—not abstract or generalized—use everyday language.

2. *Sort, shift, slash and select the "right" words that best convey what you want to say. Ask yourself, "If I live out this metaphor fully, what might be the results in my person/spiritual growth? How will it reflect my response to God? How will it reflect my response to those around me and the world at large?" (*These questions and method were used in a poetry writing class taught by poetess Luci Shaw which I attended.)

3. Be sure to keep your various pieces of writing so you can refer back to them, as an indicator of how your writing has improved as well as for ideas that may come to mind for a new piece as you review your earlier writing.

Exercise 2: Writing with Metaphors and Similes

Key: remember that the image used for either the metaphor or simile must be dissimilar from the object you are describing.

Don't write: "Her car was shiny like metal is shiny." Instead, you could write: "Her car was as shiny as a polished apple."

Choose at least four phrases from the list and write four sentences that use metaphors and four that use similes.

Here's the list: (thanks to Suzanne Rhodes for most of this list in her book *The Roar on the Other Side*.)

- A long braid of hair
- An old woman's hand

- The smell of a coming storm
- A yellow Volkswagen
- A very ripe orange
- The sound of a bulldozer
- Describe fish in a tank
- A rainstorm in the mountains
- Sheep in a pasture
- The smell of the beach

_____
_____
_____
_____
_____
_____
_____
_____
_____
_____

Extra credit: Write either a poem, short story or essay using one of the threads of thought from the list above and using as many figures of speech as possible without crowding your piece.

Exercise 3

Continue with Jill Bond's suggested assignments in *Writing to God's Glory*.

Exercise 4: Vocabulary and Word-Building

Follow the suggestions for the next set of words from Appendix E.

LESSON 4
Gathering & Planting

"The race in writing is not to the swift but to the original."
—William Zinsser, *On Writing Well*, p. 34

Section One: Words and Their Beginnings

1. In order to write well, you must become a _____.

2. Match each language to their approximate vocabulary (from Richard Lederer's *The Miracle of Language*):
   English   a. 100,000
   French   b. 130,000
   Russian   c. 615,000–two million
   German   d. 185,000

3. "_____ is a livelier tongue than _____, so use _____ words." —E.B. White

4. A good general rule for speaking and writing is with _____ and few _____.

5. What makes Anglo-Saxon words the "foundation of our language," according to Richard Lederer?

_____
_____
_____
_____

6. Perhaps the most prolific "word-crafter" of the English language was: _____.

7. Peruse the list of words invented by William Shakespeare and choose ten to use correctly in a sentence. Here's a partial list, provided by Richard Lederer: barefaced, civil tongue, cold comfort, eyesore, fancy free, foregone conclusion, foul play and fair play, green-eyed (as in jealous), heartsick, high time, hotblooded, itching palm, lackluster, laughing-stock, leapfrog, lie low, long-haired, love affair, ministering angel, pitched battle, primrose path, short shrift, snow-white, stony-hearted, tongue-tied, towering passion and yeoman's service. *The Miracle of Language*, p. 9

_____
_____
_____
_____
_____

8. Many of the phrases invented by Shakespeare have become so widely used that they are now considered _____. Here are a few, provided by Mr. Lederer: "brevity is the soul of wit; there's the rub; to thine own self be true; it smells to heaven; the very witching time of night; the primrose path; though

this be madness, yet there is method in it; dog will have his day; the apparel oft proclaims the man; neither a borrower nor a lender be; frailty, thy name is woman; something is rotten in the state of Denmark; the lady doth protest too much; to be or not to be; sweets for the sweet; to the manner born. . .,"
—*The Miracle of Language*, p. 95, 96 Can you use a few of them correctly in a brief paragraph?

_____

_____

_____

9. The _____ you choose to carry your messages determines the particulars of how you will write.

10. "Once you have reached a satisfactory degree of competence in writing _____, _____ imagery, you are ready to transfer these skills into any type of writing." —RBM

11. Good poetry and prose have a lot in common, particularly unrhymed poetry or _____ _____, which may still contain internal rhyme.

12. When skillfully used, figurative language that paints a tangible word picture can be can be worth _____.

13. Poetry that grips the emotions and conveys strong feeling has certain characteristics. Can you name some of them? Can you list some characteristics of poorly written or weak poetry writing?

_____

_____

_____

_____

_____

Section Two: Writing Well

[Much of this section's source is from *The Elements of Style* by Strunk and White. See Appendix B: Sources and Resources for more complete information.]

14. Fill in the blanks from this abbreviated list of advice on how to write well in any genre:
    a. Place _____ in the background.
    b. Write in a way that comes _____.
    c. Have a _____.

15. Writing naturally and well do not necessarily coincide. Only those who have _____ _____ _____ will be able to imitate them and succeed in writing well naturally.

16. As we have already emphasized, all good writers make proficient use of strong _____ and _____.

17. Prof. E. B. White comments: "The _____ hasn't been built that can pull a weak or inaccurate noun out of a tight place." —*The Elements of Style*, pp. 71, 72

18. He continues: "…in general, it is nouns and verbs, not their assistants, that give good writing its _____ and _____."

19. Good advice from Mrs. Morecraft: (Fill in the blanks.)
    "In order to write strong sentences, sentences that possess _____ and _____, you must expand your _____ _____. As valuable as your dictionary and thesaurus are, you must be able to bring word-treasures from the _____ of words lurking in your brain. And in order to enrich that _____, you must put words into your head from your reading and studies." —RBM

Writer Gary Provost gives excellent suggestions to improve your writing in his book *100 Ways to Improve Your Writing*. Fill in the blanks on some of them listed below:

   a. Verbs are the primary _____ _____ in your sentences. They are in charge

LESSON 4: GATHERING & PLANTING

.... If your verbs are weak, all the _____ in the world won't save your story from _____. p. 76

b. Sharpen a verb's meaning with _____ words. List some alternatives to these verbs that are more precise than the bland original word: look, throw, eat, give. p. 76

c. Use _____ voice as much as possible.
d. But use the _____ voice of the verb if you want to the emphasis to be directed towards the object receiving the action.

20. "... _____ choices must be precise and densely packed with information." —Gary Provost, p. 77

21. Remember that words have _____ that are attached to them that will either confuse or enlighten your reader.

22. _____ used wisely can enhance your writing.

23. _____ are words that describe nouns or pronouns and answer one of these questions: which one? what kind? how many?

24. _____ are words that describe a verb, an adjective or another _____ and answer one of these questions: where? when? how? how often? how long? how much?

25. True or false: A sure sign that a word is an adverb is that it ends in –ly.

_____

26. Give some examples of "awkward adverbs."

_____
_____
_____

61

27. Try using your dictionary or thesaurus and rewriting this sentence: "The black dog chased the orange cat down the road." Have fun!

_____
_____
_____
_____

28. One of the most important parts of writing, and one of the most unpopular parts, is learning to _____ and _____.

29. When you are writing with a computer, avoid _____. Hearing your fingers make sounds on the keys and seeing your thoughts on the screen in black and white can be seductive.

30. Mr. White says: "Ruthlessly delete the _____." Wordiness does not mean good writing. —*The Elements of Style*, p. 72

31. Avoid the use of _____, which Mr. White says are "leeches, sucking the blood of words." —*The Elements of Style*, p. 73

32. Give some examples of words that are "qualifiers." Hint: I know you are very good at this.

_____
_____
_____
_____

33. Sometimes writers confuse _____ with genius. These writers usually talk a lot about themselves which makes their writing uninteresting to most people.

LESSON 4: GATHERING & PLANTING

34. The journalistic writer, or news reporter, needs a checklist by which to judge the quality of his writing. What are the three items on the list?

_____
_____
_____
_____

35. Have you ever heard the acronym (look it up!) K.I.S.S.? It stands for "keep it simple, sweetheart." How does this apply to writing dialogue in a story?

_____
_____
_____
_____

36. Another good bit of advice when writing dialogue in a story or play is to read the dialogue _____ to see if it makes sense. After all, if you say, "he said," and there is more than one "he," how will the reader know who is speaking?

37. Do you love lambkins and fuzzy duckies? Well, so do I, but you should heed this advice: "Avoid the _____, the _____, and the _____. Don't be tempted by a _____–_____ word when there's a ten-center handy... The line between the _____ and the plain, between the _____ and the _____ is sometimes alarmingly fine."
—*The Elements of Style*, p. 77

38. Sometimes, it's okay to _____. "The question of the _____ is vital. Only the writer whose _____ is reliable is in a position to use bad grammar deliberately." —*The Elements of Style*, p. 77

39. "The watchword for writing is _____.... _____ is not merely a disturber of prose, it is also a destroyer of life..." —*The Elements of Style*, p. 79

63

40. Do not inject _____ unless you are writing an _____ paper.

41. Use _____ of _____ sparingly.

42. Do not take shortcuts at the cost of _____.

43. Avoid _____ _____, *n'est pas?*

44. Avoid using _____ or _____ unless you are writing dialogue where it is appropriate.

45. Avoid using _____ which will either make your writing seem dull—a dime a dozen, or boring—if you've seen one, you've seen them all.

46. Unless you're writing a television commercial or magazine ad, avoid writing in _____ _____.

47. Strunk and White close their advice on developing writing style with this observation:
"Style takes its final shape more from _____ of the mind than from _____ of _____." —*The Elements of Style*, p. 84

48. This thought reinforces what we have said several times in these classes: "As a man _____ in his heart, so is he."

Writing Exercises

Exercise 1

"... word choices must be dense and packed with information." —Gary Provost

Mr. Provost gives us these examples. After reading his examples, choose three different words (not his) and write sentences using exact, densely packed nouns that are specific, descriptive and precise. Please, use your thesaurus!

Instead of writing:	Write instead:
a black dog	a Labrador Retriever
a woman who sews	a seamstress
a man who plays piano for people	a concert pianist
cruel treatment	barbarity, savagery, brutality
happiness	joy, glee, exuberance, pleasure

Exercise 2

Read Mr. Zinsser's suggestions on how to improve your writing (see Appendix A). Choose one suggestion and write a paragraph illustrating his point.

Exercise 3

Continue working on the next pages from Jill Bond's *Writing to the Glory of God*.

Exercise 4: Vocabulary and Word-Building

Refer to the vocabulary lists in Appendix E and follow the instructions for the next set of words.

LESSON 5
Where Shall I Begin? A Few Novel Ideas for Story Starters

"Whatsoever things are true . . . honest . . . just . . . pure . . . lovely . . . of good report; if there be any virtue, and if there be any praise, think on these things." —Philippians 4:8

1. Is it Biblical to study the writings of non-believers? Why or why not? Support your answer from Mrs. Morecraft's reasons in her lecture or, if you disagree, with logical reasons from Scripture.

_____
_____
_____
_____
_____

2. Nearly every book that has seen success has one common factor. What is it?

   _____
   _____

3. Another label for the opening sentence of a story or article is the word _____.

4. Two of the best places to get ideas for stories are _____ and _____ you.

5. One of the best ways to glean story ideas is to train yourself to look at life _____ a _____ eyes.

6. "Look for the _____ and, through the _____ of your faith and knowledge..., transform the _____ into the _____." —RBM

7. God loves _____! (Annie Dillard) He is the Potter, we are the clay.

8. One of the hardest things every good writer must do is _____ and _____.

9. List as many as you can of the guidelines for good writing that were discussed for good writing. (Nine are mentioned in the lecture's listing.)

   _____
   _____
   _____
   _____
   _____

10. Some good starting points for story ideas are: _____, _____ and _____.

11. One sure way to write a good story is to use _____ you love as a guide.

12. Introductory sentences or paragraphs should "_____" the length of the story or article.

13. One good writing technique that keeps your reader interested is to _____ at incidents that will occur later in your opening paragraph.

14. Be sure to _____ your opening ideas in later paragraphs.

15. Work up to a _____ anecdote or short illustrative story in the article or short story. All other action will hinge on telling this well.

16. After this point, you are working your way towards a satisfying _____ or ending.

17. Not only the main character but also those playing a _____ role are important to the development of a good storyline.

18. Remember not to tell your story too quickly; rather, build _____.

19. Don't spell out the obvious. Let your _____ or _____ make the point.

20. "An _____ is a little story or incident that makes a point about your subject.... _____ crystallize a general idea in a specific way."
—Gary Provost

21. As you write your piece, think of yourself primarily, not as a writer but as a _____.

22. Make your reader long to know _____, and, after satisfying their desire to reach the conclusion of your story, _____ them with a fascinating, perhaps _____ ending.

23. "It's up to you, the writer, to _____ and _____, as well as inform your reader." —RBM

24. Another way to think of the structure of a good story is with the phrase: _____ beginnings and _____ endings. What does this mean?

25. Robert Frost said poetry should begin in _____ and end in _____. I reconstructed this idea a bit to say that good prose begins with _____ and ends in _____, or at least in satisfaction for the reader.

Writing Exercises

Exercise 1

During this lesson, students had the assignment of describing a room for a blind person in great detail that uses strong, sensory images other than sight. Listen to that portion of the lecture again if necessary and describe the room where you are sitting now so that a blind person could imagine it vividly.

Exercise 2

Practice writing engaging lead sentences or paragraphs for a short story or article using the list provided in the lecture:

    a. A man standing outside in a heavy rainstorm

    b. Elephants on parade

    c. A snapping turtle "stuck" in the middle of the highway

    d. A turned-over semi truck carrying a cargo that has spilled across the road

e. Sunrise in the Rockies

f. Children playing in the dirt in Haiti

g. Butterflies and baseball mitts

Exercise 3

Refer to Jill Bond's book on *Writing to God's Glory* and continue with the next section.

Exercise 4: Vocabulary and Word-Building

Continue with the next set of vocabulary words in Appendix E and follow the instructions.

LESSON 6
Journaling, Letter-Writing & E-mails—The Real You Showing Through

"We must always remember that we live *coram Deo*, before the watching face of God, and always write so that our Savior smiles at our written as well as spoken words." —RBM

1. Writing in your journal every day should be experienced as a
   _____ _____.

2. One of the earliest diaries ever published was by a man named Samuel Pepys (pronounced "peeps") who was _____.

3. List a few of the benefits of journal-writing that were mentioned in tonight's lecture:

   a. Journaling can help you learn to _____, both in terms of _____ and _____.

b. Journaling can help _____ _____ that will lead to new writing projects.

c. Journaling will help _____ your thinking processes.

d. Keeping a prayer journal will help you _____ _____ to prayer and spiritual growth.

e. Journaling provides a glimpse at _____ _____ _____ that will be a valuable document.

4. When journaling, "In every event that God sends your way, _____ _____ should be evident." —RBM

5. When forced to choose an option, choose _____ _____ as opposed to journaling about it.

6. What are some subjects that are favorites for journalists?

_____
_____
_____

7. Why journal at night?

_____
_____
_____

8. Why keep a "running journal" in your pocket throughout the day? What is the method for this kind of journaling?

_____
_____
_____

9. What are common journaling techniques? Be specific.

_____
_____
_____

10. Why should a journalist use caution in what he records?

_____
_____
_____

11. Grammar Sidebar I: Pronouns are words used in the place of _____.

12. Nouns are words that _____ people, places, things or ideas.

13. Strong nouns are specific, _____ and _____ and create a sense of _____.

14. _____ pronouns are either singular or plural: I or me, we or us, and the word you which can be either singular or plural; he, him, she, her, it or they and them.

15. _____ pronouns show something belongs to someone, different ways in which people are related and the ways in which things are related.

16. _____ pronouns are used to refer to the subject of the sentence: myself, ourselves; yourself, yourselves; himself, herself, itself or themselves.

17. _____ pronouns join a group of related words to its antecedent. They are: who, whom, whose, that and which.

18. A _____ or dependent clause is a clause that cannot stand alone. It depends on the main clause in the sentence for its meaning.

19. Write two sentences illustrating the use of a dependent or subordinate clause introduced by a relative pronoun.

_____
_____
_____
_____
_____
_____
_____
_____

20. Noteworthy aside: In Hebrew poetry, _____ is used to repeat the same thought in different words or imagery.

21. Another technique used in Hebrew poetry is that of _____ ____ _____ to emphasize its vanity when the contrasting answer is certain.

22. Relative pronouns link a subordinate clause with their own _____.

23. An antecedent is: _____.

24. Three ways to decide whether to use who or whom in a sentence:

    i. Look only at the _____ associated with the word choice.

    ii. If necessary, _____ the words to decide which fits best.

    iii. Substitute either _____ or _____ in order to make the connection easier.

25. **Grammar Sidebar II:** Word-Gathering ideas. First, keep a notebook handy and _____ your lists of words.

26. Systematize word lists both by category (e.g., a soccer game, a dance recital, a walk through the woods, a worship service, children at play, violin practice, etc.) as well as various sensory indexes. List a few of the sensory categories below along with examples.

_____
_____
_____
_____

27. In keeping categorized word lists, don't forget the _____. For instance, at the soccer game, write down as many descriptive words as possible—the teams' names, the mascots, the specific colors of everything you see, the appearance and taste of items sold at the concession stand, the yelling of the fans and so on.

_____
_____
_____
_____

28. Nobody will want to read a story or an article that lacks _____ language, beautiful _____ and appropriate _____.
Even young children can be trained to write letters. A good way for them to begin learning is by writing _____ or making simple lists.

29. When addressing an envelope, learn to gauge the _____ _____ between the lines in the address and return address, using a ruler and light marking to help at first.

30. _____ nouns should all be capitalized in the address and body of the letter. These words include titles, first and surnames, street, state and country names and names of businesses or other proper names.

31. _____ and _____ should always be checked for accuracy as well as the proper spellings of names and addresses. It's a good idea to check the address before mailing as well.

77

32. _____ _____ can be thought of as tiny collectible pieces of art.

33. Someday, someone may want to know when you wrote your letter so it's important to include the _____.

34. Before you begin your letter, address it and attach the stamp. Why is this a good idea?

_____

_____

_____

_____

35. The beginning of a letter is called the _____. The ending, just before your signature, is called the _____.

36. Express what you want to say in the _____ of the letter.

37. Never _____ _____ what you could save for another letter unless it's brief.

38. Before writing a letter ask, "To _____ am I writing?" and "_____ am I writing to them?"

39. Thinking along these lines will help you plan what to _____ in the letter.

40. Suggestions for letter-writing:

    a. Learn to write with _____ _____.

    b. Invest in beautiful _____ _____.

    c. Invest in good _____ _____.

    d. Consider _____ _____.

e. Use _____ _____ when writing.

41. Be sure to suit the _____ of the letter to its intent. Don't confuse a business and a personal letter.

42. Especially when you are writing a very personal letter, choose the _____ of everything—word, paper, pen and ink.

43. As often as possible, treat e-mails and texting as if they were _____ _____. Let the same rules apply.

44. Whether in a hand-written letter, wireless phone text or an e-mail, your writing reflects your _____ and your _____.

Writing Exercises

Exercise 1

Keep at least one journal. Devote 15-30 minutes to writing each day, simply listing the activities of your day and your reactions to them through the eyes of a Christian, or possibly add a prayer at the end of each day. You decide how to keep your journal and whether to keep more than one for different purposes. Follow the suggestions from this lecture as much as possible and remember that your grandchildren may read this someday so use caution when expressing personal ideas and opinions.

Exercise 2

Experiment with the idea of writing a short story or play using a fabricated journal or diary as the vehicle. Read some of the journals, collected letters and diaries in the reading list in Appendix B (look for the section entitled Suggested Reading for Collections of Letters and Journals) and imitate their styles in your journal, story or play.

Exercise 3

During the next few days, devote a page in your notebook for each separate activity you encounter: babysitting, cooking, sewing, a sport, watching people at an airport, a skill, a craft or hobby and so on. On each page, write the heading of the subject at the top and make lists of specific words, phrases and technical terms having to do with that subject. Finally, write a story or journalistic article about that activity or area of interest that skillfully incorporates your collected words and phrases. Have fun!

Exercise 4

Write a number of different letters that incorporate the suggestions mentioned in this lecture—a business letter or an e-mail, personal letters of gratitude or encouragement, letters to your parents or relatives. Try to use "the best words in the best ways" as you express your beautiful thoughts in beautiful words on lovely paper using careful writing techniques.

Exercise 5

Continue with the next assignment in Jill Bond's book *Writing to God's Glory*.

Exercise 6: Vocabulary and Word-Building

Continue with the next section of words in Appendix E as you follow the instructions.

LESSON 7
Digging Deeper—Common Writing Errors

"It is an old observation that the best writers sometimes disregard the rules of rhetoric. When they do so, however, the reader will usually find in the sentence some compensating merit, attained at the cost of the violation. Unless he is certain of doing as well, he will probably do best to follow the rules. After he has learned, by their guidance, to write plain English adequate for everyday uses, let him look for the secrets of style to the study of the masters of literature."
—William Strunk, Jr., from the introduction to *The Elements of Style*

The following list of common writing errors was taken from *Webster's Pocket Grammar Dictionary*:

1. The dictionary definition of words is referred to as _____ while associations that carry emotional weight relating to a word are called _____.

2. When writing dialogue, be careful not to use too much _____.

3. Why is that a good suggestion?

   _____
   _____
   _____
   _____

4. Which is the correct meaning of the word aggravate? a.) to increase b.) to irritate

5. Can the contraction *ain't* ever be properly used when writing? _____

6. Explain the difference in meaning between *among* and *between*.

   _____
   _____
   _____
   _____

7. *As good as* and *better than* are _____.

8. Applying the rules learned concerning these words, give a correct example of usage.

   _____
   _____
   _____

9. The combination of these words, *as yet*, is _____. Omit *as* for the correct usage.

10. The misuse of the word *badly* instead of the correct words _____ _____ occurs frequently.

11. When referring to nurturing children in the home, the best verbs are either _____ or _____ _____ rather than *raise* which is more associated with nurturing vegetables.

12. The too frequent use of *but* as a conjunction leads to a succession of
    _____ _____ that over-use connective words.

13. What characterizes paragraphs built by weak writers who over-use connective words?

    _____
    _____
    _____
    _____

14. What is Mr. Strunk's suggestion to correct this type of weak writing?

    _____
    _____
    _____

15. A _____ sentence is a sentence that is not grammatically complete until the final clause or phrase.

16. It is the opposite of a _____ sentence, where the subject and verb are introduced at the beginning.

17. *Claim* is a strong word that should not be used in the place of _____.

18. Give an example of the correct usage of the word *claim*.

    _____
    _____
    _____

19. "Use _____ verbs unless there is no comfortable way to get around a passive verb." —Zinsser, p. 67

20. "A style that consists of passive constructions will _____ the reader's energy." —Zinsser, p. 67

21. Most of the time, writers should choose _____ words rather than _____ ones.

22. Anglo-Saxon words are _____ and _____, whereas words with Latin origins are long and more ambiguous.

23. "_____ are the most important of all your tools." —Zinsser, p. 67

24. "Make _____ verbs activate your sentences and avoid the kind that need an appended _____ to complete their work." —Zinsser, p. 67

25. Too long a sentence? What to do?

_____

_____

_____

26. "Use _____ _____ as you would pepper flakes in food. ....make sure [they] are scattered effectively throughout your writing in places that are entirely appropriate; otherwise, they lose their 'zing.'" —Zinsser, p. 68

27. "Know how to use _____ to the best advantage." —Zinsser, p. 68

28. Learn how to use words that effectively _____ _____ in your paper, story or article.

29. List some of those words and phrases that gracefully shift gears or lead into a new thought.

_____
_____
_____
_____

30. Mr. Zinsser terms these words _____ _____.

31. It's always important to _____ your reader so you don't lose him in the flow of time changes by using words like *yesterday*, *meanwhile* or other time-related words.

32. _____ pronouns (such as she, he or I) are used as subjects of sentences.

33. _____ pronouns (such as her, him or me) are used as objects in sentences.

34. Correctly use both **subjective** and **objective** pronouns in two sentences, first with a simple subject and object and then another sentence with a compound subject and compound object. For instance, "Mother saw me waving." "Mother and I saw her waving." Then, "Mother and I saw Bill and her waving."

_____
_____
_____

35. Poetic terms: _____ means "bad sound." Some examples are words such as screech, scold, wrestle, grumble, tremble, topple, boom, shrill, shriek, scream. —Suzanne Rhodes, *The Roar on the Other Side*

36. Many of these words have _____ stacked together giving them a harder sound.

37. _____ is the opposite term and includes words that are harmonious, pleasing to the ear. Some examples are words such as praise, pray, smile, peace, bee, lamb, veil, morning, summer, slimmer, glow, wing, lake, ocean and so on.

38. In these words, we notice drawn-out _____ sounds that contrast sharply with our previous list.

39. A type of word used to create sound effects in writing is called _____. Some examples are: hiss, buzz, gurgle, crackle, tinkle, giggle, jingle.

40. A device used to incorporate internal rhyme in poems is called _____. In this technique, vowel sounds within close proximity are repeated. Examples: feed/sheet, stick/lift, boot/moon.

41. _____ moves the similarity of sound to the ends of words such as shock/cheek, fallen/melon, voyage/sewage, wave/love. _____, not spelling, is the defining factor here.

42. In _____, repetition of initial and/or internal consonants is employed. This technique was used widely in ancient times to aid bards and story-tellers in _____. Some examples are: rascals wrestling in the road and follow the sailor to Manila; and from "Sir Gawain and the Green Knight", And in guise all of green, the gear and the man: a coat cut close that clung to his sides…

43. The most familiar kind of sound effect used in poetry is _____.

44. _____ _____ employs sounds that are exactly the same except for the initial consonants such as like/bike, girl/squirrel, boy/toy.

45. _____ _____ is another name for this rhyming scheme.

46. Rhyming words found within the line are described as using _____ _____ as in, "All seared with trade; bleared, smeared with toil."

47. Mrs. Rhodes says end rhymes have lost much of their appeal in the 20th century because they often have lost their _____ and achieved the level of _____.

48. What is another legitimate reason not to use end rhymes in a poem?

_____

_____

_____

Writing Exercises

Exercise 1

Here's the paragraph quoted early in our lesson from Mr. Strunk's book, along with his commentary.

> "The third concert of the subscription series was given last evening, and a large audience was in attendance. Mr. Edward Appleton was the soloist, and the Boston Symphony Orchestra furnished the instrumental music. The former showed himself to be an artist of the first rank, while the latter proved itself fully deserving of its high reputation. The interest aroused by the series has been very gratifying to the Committee, and it is planned to give a similar series annually hereafter. The fourth concert will be given on Tuesday, May, 10, when an equally attractive programme will be presented." —Strunk, *The Elements of Style*, p. 26.

Why is this considered weak writing? There is nothing grammatically incorrect about the structure of the sentences. Mr. Strunk points out, "apart from its triteness and emptiness, the paragraph ... is weak because of the structure of its sentences, with their mechanical symmetry and sing-song. Contrast with them the sentences.

. . in any piece of good English prose." p. 26. [In the lecture, we contrasted this poorly written paragraph with a well-written one from D. Martyn-Lloyd Jones' book *Spiritual Depression*.]

Mr. Strunk gives us good suggestions about how to correct this type of weak writing. He says, ". . .recast enough of them [the weak sentences] to remove the monotony, replacing them by simple sentences, by sentences of two clauses joined by a semi-colon ... whichever best represent the real relations of the thought."
—Strunk, *The Elements of Style*, p. 26

Take the weak paragraph above as a writing assignment and re-write it as a more interesting and informative news article. Next, take what you've learned from this exercise and write a brief news item relevant to your life—a church function, a sporting event, a craft fair—anything that you choose. Have fun!

Exercise 2

Write a poem employing some of the poetic devices we discussed. Make sure your poem doesn't sound like "sawdust and sand." Remember that poetry aims to delight as well as instruct.

Exercise 3

Continue with the next assignment in Jill Bond's book *Writing to God's Glory*.

Exercise 4: Vocabulary and Word-Building

Continue with the next section of the vocabulary lists in Appendix E.

LESSON 8
Checking Your Tools—Packing Up to Go

"And fare thee well, my own true love, and fare thee well awhile; but I will come again, my dear, though it were ten-thousand miles, though it were ten-thousand miles." —Robert Burns, from "My Love is Like the Red, Red Rose"

Review and Renew

As I go back over some of the main points from the past seven lessons, I hope you claim many of my suggestions as your own and notice vast improvements as you write.

Here's a little review from week one with a few of my favorite themes picked up for review. By the way, there are no answers for these questions in the answer key—you're on your own!:

- Why should you strive to be a skillful writer as a Christian?
- What does it mean to "write to God's glory"?
- What results from a lazy, careless lifestyle as it applies to your writing?

- What impact should studying Scripture have on your writing?
- Of what importance is tracing the history of redemption to you?
- Why is it important to see God's hand of providence in history and in your life and times?
- Why should you never walk away from challenges God puts in your path?
- Why should you record God's mighty acts of providence in your own life?
- What relevance does Psalm 145:3, 4 have to you and what you write?
- Ephesians 2:10 reads: "For we are His workmanship, created in Christ Jesus unto good works, which God hath before ordained that we should walk in them." How else can we translate the word in this verse that says we are God's workmanship?
- What does that mean in your own life and in reference to your writing?

Another theme of this lesson was book recommendations. I hope you will take advantage of the many books I recommended by using lists from trusted friends as well as some of my own personal preferences in Appendix B and Appendix D. These are available on my blog (**becky-gracenotes.blogspot.com**—in an archived section) as well as in this lecture.

During our previous session we referenced the winning list of writing contestants. Of lasting relevance to you is the judging criteria. I hope you will take time to read over the list and apply some of these principles to your own writing efforts. Here's the list.

Criteria Employed for Judging the Writing Contest Entries

- Grammatical accuracy
- Strong, imaginative imagery that avoided using tired, trite phrases, jargon or slang
- Good lead sentences and first paragraphs, where applicable
- Clearly understood development of the theme or thesis, where applicable
- A strong concluding paragraph
- Good sentence structure with strong nouns, verbs and properly used modifiers
- For rhyming poems, strict adherence to the chosen meter

- For unrhymed poems, strong, palpable imagery appropriate to the subject and additionally,
- Skillful use of internal rhyme
- Interesting themes for both poetry and prose
- Did the writing grab and keep our interest throughout, or was the piece,
- Too rhetorical (instructional with little to keep interest in a storyline)
- Too artificial (either too silly and unbelievable or impossible situations)
- Too boring
- Too "wordy"?
- With articles and essays, did the writer make and prove a point well?
- If a song, was the meter adhered to throughout? Was the imagery strong? Did the words fit the tune and was the music appropriate to the message?
- In all types of writing, did the writer strike a chord with us so that we wanted to keep reading and felt satisfied when we finished reading it—either entertained, inspired, or in some other way glad we had read it? Or was the piece easy to put down, even before the end? Did we enjoy reading the poem, story, essay, article or song?

This final point is always the deciding factor when judging a piece of writing. If your writing compels us to keep reading, holds our interest and leaves us wanting more, your submission has more potential than a piece that may be written more correctly, following all the rules, but doesn't sufficiently inspire or instruct us. Remember that writing should delight as well as inform.

All writing errors can be corrected. All writers can improve. Don't be discouraged if your name doesn't make it into the winner's circle or to the list of honorable mentions. Keep at it! Journal, write and re-write your poems, stories, essays, articles and papers. Give them to your parents and friends to critique and ask for suggestions for improvement. Keep reading great books and take note of good sentence structure, strong nouns and verbs and effectively placed modifiers. Notice how successful writers describe scenes full of emotion, how they write dialogue and the skills employed in creating tangible, palpable imagery. Do good story writers use mostly long or short words and sentences? Pay attention and imitate great writing styles; but at the same time strive to write with your own "voice." Think about what makes a book or story memorable. As you read, take notes on all these topics—this is perhaps the best way to improve your own writing.

Don't be afraid of criticism. In fact, ask for it all the time. Ask anyone who will read or listen to your writing, "Does that make sense to you? What do I need to add? What do I need to take out? How could this be written to convey my point better? Do I need to re-write or just start over?"

You will never improve as a runner if you don't run or as a singer if you don't sing. You will never become a better writer if you only practice writing skills occasionally. Write every day. Read every day. Ask the Lord to help you improve your writing for His glory and He will.

Soli Deo Gloria,
Mrs. Rebecca B. Morecraft

Volume II

Introduction to Volume II Study Guide

I hope this course will prompt you to search hungrily for vocabulary boosters, words, phrases and ideas that will propel you into the future on wings of knowledge and imagination! May I remind you that you will get out of these classes almost exactly what you are willing to put into them? If you only listen to each lesson and jot down a note or two or chuckle at the corny jokes I toss at you, you will probably leave this course unchanged. But if you buckle down and work, vistas for improved self-expression as you write and speak will open for you, and you will find yourself forever changed in many good ways. That is my prayer, my hope, my goal for each of you.

Mrs. Rebecca B. Morecraft
Canton, GA
June 28, A.D. 2011

LESSON 1
The Soup Course—Grammar Served Up with a Sprig of Parsley

"No one who cooks, cooks alone. Even at her most solitary, a cook in the kitchen is surrounded by generations of cooks past, the advice and menus of cooks present, and the wisdom of cookbook writers." —Laurie Colwin, quoted in *A Return to Sunday Dinner,* by Russell Cronkhite

1. When we take a dish or a sentence apart so that each element can be expertly analyzed and appreciated, we _____ it.

2. An important part of skillful writing as well as effective cooking is choosing the best _____ and knowing how to use them.

3. _____ can have a powerful effect for generations to come.

4. Just as a meal should be nutritious and pleasing to the eyes, even so our written and spoken words should be _____ and _____.

5. Jesus is referred to metaphorically in the Bible as the _____ of life, that Food that is necessary to spiritual health.

6. In *Pilgrim at Tinker Creek*, author Annie Dillard states that God loves _____!

7. What do you think she means? How does this idea apply to writing and meal preparation?

_____

_____

_____

_____

8. A _____ is a group of words that makes a statement.

9. The _____ of a sentence is that which is being talked about, the main ingredient.

10. Technically, the _____ of a sentence is a word or group of words that names the person or thing about whom or which the statement is made.

11. A subject, in its simple form, is either a _____ (or a group of words acting as a _____), or a _____.

12. The _____ is what is said about the subject and is a word or group of words that makes a statement about the subject.

13. The predicate, in its simple form, is a _____ alone but will always contain a _____.

14. There are four categories of sentences:

    a. a _____ sentence makes a statement.

    b. an _____ sentence asks a question.

    c. an _____ sentence issues a command, makes a request or gives instructions.

    d. an _____ sentence expresses strong emotion.

15. Often, when no subject is present, the pronoun you is the subject and is called the _____ subject.

16. I Corinthians 10:31 reminds us that God is the understood Subject of our lives as Christians when it says, "So then, whether you eat or drink or _____ you do, do it all to the glory of God."

17. _____ are the parts of a sentence that explain or better identify the main words.

18. _____ answer questions about the subject or the predicate.

19. _____ modify nouns or pronouns and answer the questions: Which one? What kind? How many?

20. _____ modify verbs, adjectives or other _____ and answer these questions: How? When? Where? Why? Under what circumstances? How much? How often? To what extent?

21. We call the subject of the sentence and the words that modify, explain or describe it the _____ _____.

22. The predicate of the sentence and all the words that modify, explain or further describe it is called the _____ _____.

23. _____ give us names—of people, places, objects, ideas or states of being. Give some examples of each classification.

_____
_____

24. _____ nouns are names for all the members of a class of persons or things. Give some examples.

_____
_____

25. _____ nouns are names that designate individual members of a class. List some examples.

_____
_____

26. _____ _____ nouns name a group of persons or things. Give examples.

_____
_____

27. _____ _____ nouns specify which group of persons or things are being referred to. Give examples.

_____
_____

28. The main uses of nouns are these: (After identifying them, write some examples of your own.)

   a. As the _____ of the verb. "Trees grow."

   b. As the _____ _____ of the verb. "He wrote the letter."

   c. As the _____ _____ of the verb. "He gave the boy an orange."

   d. As the _____ of a _____. "I came from home."

   e. As a _____ _____. "Mrs. Morecraft is a writer."

   f. As an _____. "Mrs. Morecraft, our teacher, loves cherries."

   g. In _____ _____. "Boys, go clean your room."

29. Other characteristics of nouns (and pronouns) include these: (Please write some examples of each characteristic using both nouns and pronouns where possible.)

   a. _____ indicates how many persons or things are designated.

   b. _____ indicates whether the object named is male, female, neuter or common.

   c. A noun is said to be in first, second or third _____, indicating either the speaker or those associated with him.

   d. Nouns have three cases, determined by their use in a sentence:

      i. The _____ case, used to name things or persons or ideas and used as the subject of a sentence, phrase or clause. Write an example.

      _____

      _____

      ii. The _____ case, written in the same form as the former case but used as an object of the verb. Write an example.

      _____

      _____

iii. The _____ case, indicated by adding an apostrophe to indicate ownership. Give an example.

_____

_____

30. Most English words form plurals by adding an ____ to the end. Examples, please.

_____

_____

_____

_____

31. There are approximately six singular noun endings that require an –*es* to form the plural. What are those endings? Give some examples.

_____

_____

_____

_____

32. As with most spelling rules in English, there are some additions to the rule just stated. What are some words that require an additional –*z* before adding the –*es*?

_____

_____

_____

33. Why is it correct to say "a cookie," (because cookie begins with a consonant), and "an egg" (because egg begins with a vowel), but incorrect to say "a –s"?

_____
_____
_____
_____

34. Please review the remainder of rules for making nouns plural and attempt to memorize as many as you can. Remember, the more technical information you can store in your brain, the less frequently you'll have to look things up! That's a great boon to help your writing flow rather than become choppy and disconnected.

35. A _____ is a word that joins words in a sentence and comes in three varieties:

   a. _____ _____ : but, or, yet, so, for, and, and nor. "BOYSFAN" is the mnemonic word used to remember them.

   b. _____ _____: These are lonely words that must have a relative nearby, usually in the same sentence. Both/and, either/or, neither/nor, not only/also, and not only/but also.

   c. _____ _____: These are used in the beginning of dependent clauses (clauses with a subject and verb that cannot stand alone). After, although, as if, as in, as long as, as much as, as soon as, assuming that, because, before, even though, how, if, in order that, in that, inasmuch as, now that ... and many more.

36. An _____ is a word that expresses strong emotions, surprise or pain.

37. The functions of the common comma are to grammar like musical notation is to song, pointing out "_____, _____, _____, _____ and _____."
—Lynne Truss, *Eats, Shoots and Leaves*, p. 70

38. Comma usage: the comma is correct if it can be replaced by the word _____ or _____.

39. In American usage, the _____ or serial comma is more common than in Great Britain.

40. What is an "Oxford comma"?

_____
_____

41. Give an example.

_____
_____
_____
_____

42. Whether you decide to use the Oxford/serial or not, one rule should apply: _____ _____.

43. One common writing error is the _____ _____, or joining two independent clauses with a conjunction, separating them with a comma. This is also sometimes called a _____ sentence.

44. Give an example of a comma splice and then repair it.

_____
_____
_____
_____

45. Commas used to _____ act like brackets or parentheses, giving the reader additional information that is unnecessary to the basic sentence.

46. If you don't have a _____ _____ use a comma, don't!

Writing Exercises

Exercise 1

Renee DeGroot states in her book *Health for Godly Generations*:

> "Everything we do is inescapably religious. We eat either for God's glory or for fleshly pleasure. Will we be righteous or humanistic, serving God or man?" p. 47

Think about this statement in terms of 1 Corinthians 10:31: "So then, whether you eat or drink or whatever you do, do it all to the glory of God."

Now think of the wide variety of delicious foods God has given us to sample and write a convincing short article explaining why it's alright to eat your favorite food. Try to use good logical reasons as well as carefully chosen, interesting words. Be sure to remember the various rules of grammar and punctuation we've discussed. Have fun!

Exercise 2

Take the quote below as your basic assumption and argue the case for learning the sticky details of grammar. Limit yourself to a few short paragraphs.

> "Grammar isn't the only key to good sentence writing, of course. Word choice, common sense, passion, information—all these elements and more are essential. ... Yet all great writing has one thing in common. It starts with a sentence. The sentence is a microcosm of any written work, and understanding it means understanding writing itself—how to structure ideas, how to emphasize what's important, how to make practical use of grammar, how to cut the [unnecessary], and, above all, how to serve the almighty Reader." —June Casagrande, *It Was the Best of Sentences, It Was the Worst of Sentences*, p. 6

Exercise 3

Continue working through the instruction and assignments in Jill Bond's book *Writing to God's Glory*.

Exercise 4

Add the next set of vocabulary words from Appendix E to your list. Be sure to follow the guidelines set down at the beginning of the lists.

LESSON 2
The Appetizer Course—Speaking & Writing with Agility & Grace

"The pleasantest hours of our life are all connected by a more or less tangible link with some memory of the table." —Charles Pierre Monselet, quoted in *A Return to Sunday Dinner,* by Russell Cronkhite

1. All literary works have one thing in common: they begin with a _____.

2. What makes a good sentence? The list could include keeping the reader's _____, with a variety of both _____ and _____ sentences that contain _____ _____ information and tangible _____.

3. Avoid these pitfalls in writing strong sentences:

   a. Sentences that are too _____

   b. Sentences that are too _____

   c. The grammar was _____

   d. The information was _____

   e. The writing was trying too hard to _____

   f. There was too much _____

   g. The sentence was _____

   h. There were many _____ words

   i. There was nothing _____ about the story line

   j. The language used was too 'hip' and full of _____

   k. The information given was wrong or historically _____

   l. The writer tried to give too much _____

   m. The writer forgot his _____

4. You should write with the reader's _____ in mind.

5. Avoid writing in complicated sentences containing _____ _____.

6. Avoid word choices that are _____ rather than _____.

7. Use _____ rather than _____ imagery.

8. _____ clauses are introduced by the relative pronouns which, that, who or whom.

9. Avoid _____ _____ without adequate or pertinent information in them.

10. Words are meant to convey _____, _____, inspire _____, proliferate _____ _____, move to _____ and cause _____ _____, but never to bruise unnecessarily, discourage or misinform.

11. Words, even more than bows and arrows, can destroy a man or woman by _____ _____ _____.

12. _____–_____ agreement describes the use of the correct verb form that corresponds with its subject.

13. Nouns and pronouns can be identified according to person, case and gender. Verbs can be identified as past, present or future tense which indicates _____.

14. Confusion about which verb tense to use usually occurs because of _____ _____ between the real subject of the sentence and its verb.

15. When both halves of a _____ _____ are singular, so is the verb.

16. The rule for mixed compound subjects (where one word is singular and the other plural) for verb agreement is this: if the part nearer the verb is singular, the verb is _____ and if plural, then the verb is _____. Give an example.

_____
_____
_____

17. Words that stand for _____ of things require a singular verb. Key: Can you use the article *the* before the word? Then it's singular. If you need to use the article *a* with of after the word, it's plural.

18. If the word _____ stands for one thing, use a singular verb. If it stands for several things, use a plural verb. Give examples.

_____
_____
_____

19. When a statement starts with _____, the verb can be either singular or plural because _____ is a _____ subject.

20. Look in the sentence that begins with the word _____ for the real subject in order to decide on verb tense.

21. When we speak wishfully, "I wish I _____," is the correct verb tense. This is called the _____ mood.

22. The British call the period an _____ _____.

23. If a sentence ends with an abbreviation that has a final period, do you add another one? _____

24. If a sentence ends in an ellipsis (three dots that indicate omission), is one more period added? Why or why not?

_____
_____
_____

25. If a sentence concludes with a title of a work that ends in a question mark or an exclamation, do or don't add a final period?

_____
_____

26. If a sentence has a smaller sentence within it (surrounded by dashes or parentheses), do or don't use a period to end the "inside" sentence?

_____
_____
_____

27. Can you give examples of the rules in 23-26 above?

_____
_____
_____
_____
_____
_____
_____
_____
_____

28. _____ clauses only need commas to set them off if they are introductory.

29. If you include any _____ _____—during, while, before, after, when, because—introductory usages of adverbial clauses beginning with one of the conjunctions listed above would need a comma to set off the clause. On the other hand, if you use those _____ after an independent clause, then you do NOT use a comma.

Examples:

"Bob likes candy and Jane likes broccoli."

"While Jane likes broccoli, she loves candy."

"Bob does not eat second helpings because he loves ice cream after dinner."

Writing Exercises

Exercise 1

Take your cue from this quotation from the Harris brothers' online newsletter of February 3, 2011: "We must train ourselves to feel pleasure, liking, disgust, and hatred at those things which really are pleasant, likeable, disgusting, and hateful. We must constantly ask ourselves whether the things we put before our eyes train us in this way, or just further distort our ability to appreciate [what is] good, true, and beautiful."

Write a three-paragraph defense and explanation of this comment, incorporating the rules of good sentence structure learned from this lecture. Have fun!

Exercise 2

Richard Lederer asks that we learn "not only to talk, but to communicate." What do you think he means by this sentence? How does his next comment more fully explain the first one? "May our thoughts and aspirations become words that serve to build bridges from mind to mind and from heart to heart, creating a fellowship of those who would hold fast to that which is good" (Lederer, *The Miracle of Language*, p. 243). Why should Christian writers embrace this idea? Write three paragraphs that explain your ideas as they relate to these statements using good sentence structure and grammar. Have fun!

Exercise 3

Continue with assignments from Jill Bond's book *Writing to God's Glory*.

Exercise 4

Study the next vocabulary words from the lists in Appendix E.

LESSON 3
The Salad Course—Tossing Together Clear Thinking with Clean Writing
(or how to clearly state your thoughts without overdoing the dressing)

"In the childhood memories of every good cook, there's a large kitchen, a warm stove, a simmering pot and a mom." —Barbara Costikyan, quoted in *Return to Sunday Dinner,* by Russell Cronkhite

1. Unless you have a deadline, it's often easier to see your mistakes if you _____.

2. A checklist for proofing your writing could include these items:

   a._____

b._____

c._____

d._____

e._____

f._____

g._____

h._____

i._____

3. A good baseline question when you proof-read is this one: Is my _____ really a _____?

4. Review the definition of a sentence: A complete sentence must have a _____ and a _____.

5. In order to have a sentence that communicates, you need to make sure the "ingredients" are correctly _____.

6. A _____ is a group of words that does not contain a subject and a verb.

7. A _____ must have a subject and a verb.

8. An _____ clause can stand alone as a complete sentence. Give an example.

_____

_____

_____

_____

LESSON 3: THE SALAD COURSE—TOSSING TOGETHER CLEAR THINKING WITH CLEAN WRITING

9. A _____ clause must be connected to a complete sentence, even though it has a subject and a verb. Give an example.

_____
_____
_____
_____

10. Most likely, your _____ will tell you whether a clause is dependent or independent.

11. When planning a dinner menu for guests, several considerations should come to mind. Can you name some of them?

_____
_____

12. Some of these same principles apply to writing. Can you name some of them?

_____
_____

13. A sentence fragment is _____.

14. Sometimes, sentence fragmentation can be corrected with the use of the _____. Can you give an example?

_____
_____
_____
_____

15. Sentence fragments are "legal" in three instances:

    a. For _____ "Are you sure?" he asked. "Yes!" she replied. "I am certain."

    b. In informal _____ "Full?" asked Sue. "Ugh, ate too much."

    c. When using _____ and _____ "Absolutely not!" "Why?" "Because..."

16. Periods are usually inserted in abbreviations of certain categories and not others. Here's a list of both—write the letter "A" beside those categories which should include periods in their abbreviated forms and "NA" beside those which do not include periods. Write two examples for each category.

    a. Months _____

    _____
    _____

    b. States _____

    _____
    _____

    c. Days of the week _____

    _____
    _____

    d. Agencies, companies and organizations _____

    _____
    _____

e. Titles, either earned degrees or elected or appointed status
   _____

_____

_____

f. Computer terms _____

_____

_____

g. Addresses (streets, lanes, etc.) _____

_____

_____

h. Measurements _____

_____

_____

i. Countries _____

_____

_____

j. Educational tests _____

_____

_____

k. Radio/television stations and networks _____

_____

_____

l. Medical terminology _____
_____
_____

m. Directions _____
_____
_____

n. Chemical elements _____
_____
_____

o. Latitude/longitude _____
_____
_____

p. Latin terms _____
_____
_____

17. _____ _____ are used at the end of interrogative sentences which ask questions or indicate uncertainty or doubt.

18. _____ _____ are used for high energy sentences and should be used rarely.

19. _____ _____ are like spices–if you use too many of them it will be like eating a salad with too much dressing.

20. _____–_____ words are the strongest words in the English language.

21. Rev. Edward Everett Hale gave advice on writing. His writing style was described as being _____, _____ and vivacious.

22. His advice on how to write included these remarks:

    a. "Know what _____."

    b. Secondly, he advised: _____ _____.

    c. Third: always use _____ _____ _____.

    d. Fourth: A ____ word is better than a _____ _____.

23. "If your every-day language is not fit for a letter or for print, it is not _____ for _____." —E. E. Hale

24. Be careful when quoting someone, whether _____ or _____. Get the quote exactly right and give credit where credit is due.

25. If you use someone's written or spoken words and don't give them credit, you are guilty of _____ which is a form of theft, for which you could be legally liable.

26. _____ _____ are used to enclose the exact words a person said in the exact order in which he spoke them.

27. We call this kind of sentence a _____ quotation.

28. An _____ quotation simply tells what was said without employing exact words.

29. Quotation marks should be used when the speakers change in _____ _____.

30. If you are quoting several sentences by someone, wait till the _____ of the monologue to place the end quotation mark.

31. If you have a long quote of more than one paragraph, put _____ quotation marks at the _____ of each new paragraph and _____ quotation marks only at the end.

32. Use quotation marks to enclose titles of short works such as short _____, _____, titles of _____, _____, chapters from _____, _____ and _____ of videos, television or radio programs.

33. _____, technical _____, or other expressions that are outside normal usage should be enclosed in _____ _____.

34. _____, _____ _____ _____ go inside closing quotation marks; _____ and _____ go outside the closing quotation marks in American usage.

35. One rule that can be confusing: _____ _____ _____ _____ can go either inside or outside the closing quotation marks, depending on what is being quoted.

36. If what is being quoted is a question, the question mark goes _____ the closing quotation mark. Give an example.

_____

_____

_____

_____

37. If the quotation doesn't form a question, but the sentence as a whole does, the question mark goes _____ the closing quotation mark. Give an example.

_____

_____

_____

_____

38. The same rules apply to _____ _____.

39. When double quotation marks are already being used and you need to set something off inside a sentence, such as a book title or another quotation, use _____ quotation marks.

40. **Elocution principles:** In Swinton's *Fifth Reader and Speaker*, published in 1883, "elocution" is defined as: "The art of uttering _____, either in speaking or reading, with all agreeableness, feeling, force and effect of which their meaning is susceptible."

41. Mr. Swinton says that good reading [aloud] depends on the proper use of the following:

    a. Force and _____

    b. Time

    c. Pitch

    d. Inflections or slides

    e. Quality

    f. Emphasis

42. He also states that, "Good reading presupposes correct _____ in which term are included: articulation, syllabication and accent."

43. By "force," Mr. Swinton means the degree of _____ or _____ used in vocal utterance.

44. The varied degree of force can be correlated with _____ terminology.

45. _____ in speaking or reading aloud refers to the manner of applying emphatic force in the utterance of a syllable.

46. This term is distinguished from force as denoted by the mode in which force is rendered impressive in ____ ____.

47. The three principal varieties of stress are:

    a. _____, or the root, with the force applied at the beginning of a vowel

    b. _____, in which there is an increase of force towards the middle of a vowel

    c. _____, with the force applied at the close of a vowel

48. One common error in writing to avoid is the use of worn-out _*Cliches*_. Can you list some that are commonly used both in speech and writing? Avoid them like the plague.

_____
_____
_____
_____

Writing Exercises

Exercise 1

Try your hand at writing a paragraph that contains combinations of longer and shorter sentences with both independent and dependent clauses in them. Try separating your longer sentences into two shorter ones. Take some of the shorter sentences and try combining them (logically) with other shorter sentences. Take an interesting subject for the theme of your paragraph and make it as convincing and attention-grabbing as possible.

Think about the clichés you listed in 48 above. Use them as the theme of a paragraph that substitutes better phrases and imagery. For instance, instead of writing: "The little girl was as pretty as a picture, as cute as a button and as gentle as a lamb," you could write: "Mary wasn't your typical four-year-old. Most children her age come across as thoughtless of others, rowdy or shy. Instead, Mary displayed a gentle and quiet spirit. Her hazel eyes took in the needs of the other children as she tried to make them feel at home, dimpled cheeks smiling and blond curls bouncing with her enthusiasm." Have fun!

Exercise 2

Using words from Appendix E in this study guide or words of your own choosing, write a poem or short story that employs only one syllable words. You can do it! Send your results to me at **mrs.morecraft@gmail.com**. I'd love to see what you accomplish! (For inspiration, look at the poem by Joseph Addison Alexander, "The Power of Short Words," in the quotations section of this Study Guide in Appendix A.)

Exercise 3

Continue to follow the instruction and assignments from Jill Bond's *Writing to God's Glory*.

Exercise 4

Follow the instructions for the next set of vocabulary words from Appendix E.

LESSON 4
The Main Course—Writing a Sentence that Satisfies

"There is no better time or place to build friendships than around the joy-filled, warm, and inviting table we set for friends on Sunday."
—Russell Cronkhite, *A Return to Sunday Dinner*

1. When preparing a meal, writing a note or an essay, the best way to assure that nothing is left out that you meant to include is to _____ a _____.

2. One characteristic that we find lacking in today's culture is lack of _____.

3. "_____" is an adjective modifying the name of the person in the greeting of a letter and requiring a comma after it, while "Hi" or "Hello" or any other greeting you choose will not need a comma because these words are viewed as interjections.

4. "If you strive to increase both your working and your reading vocabulary, you will be _____ _____ to understand the thinking and writing of both past and present generations and be like the sons of Issachar, "men who _____ _____ _____, with knowledge of what Israel should do" (I Chronicles 12:32). —RBM

5. What are three excellent reasons we discussed for expanding your vocabulary?

   a. If you have a wide vocabulary, your _____ _____ will be ahead of the game–you will grasp _____ and instantly "translate" the meaning of the words into your comfort zone.

   b. You will be better able to _____ _____ in more cogent terms. In other words, you will learn to be _____ and _____.

   c. Your brain will begin to make vocabulary _____ that allows you to write with deeper and broader _____. This is why _____ is so important.

6. _____ deals with the origin or derivation of words.

7. When you know the meaning of the _____ of a word, for example Latin, you can better understand and more easily remember all the words built on this _____.

8. "Learn one _____ and you have the key that will unlock the meanings of up to ten or twenty words in which the _____ appears." —Norman Lewis, *Word Power Made Easy*, p. xx

9. In the _____ approach to vocabulary building, says Mr. Lewis, you will learn:

   a. about _____, roots and _____;

   b. to figure out unfamiliar words by recognizing their _____, the building blocks from which they are constructed;

   c. to _____ words correctly by learning to put these building blocks together in the proper way;

d. to derive _____ from nouns, nouns and _____ from adjectives, adjectives from _____, etc., and do all this correctly.

10. "Learn how to deal with _____ and you will feel comfortable with words—you will use new words with self-assurance—you will be able to figure out thousands of words you hear or read even if you have never heard or seen these words before." —Norman Lewis, *Word Power Made Easy*, p. xx, xxi

11. As a general rule, all _____ should be as close as possible to the word they describe.

12. One of the most common problems with misplaced modifiers comes with what are called _____ modifiers—words like almost, even, hardly, just, merely, nearly, only, scarcely and simply.

13. _____ modifiers have no word or phrase close by them. Incorrect: "Tiny ears hidden, Jane wondered how the dog could hear." Correctly written: "Jane wondered how the dog could hear with such tiny ears hidden under thick fur."

14. A modifier left in the middle of a sentence could easily modify nouns on either side of it. This poor construction is called a _____ modifier. Can you give an example and then correct it?

_____

_____

_____

_____

15. Good sentence construction will observe the rules of _____ construction, like an isosceles triangle with at least two sides created equal.

16. Observing the rules of _____ construction means that you write all the similar parts of a sentence in the same way.

17. Observing the rules of _____ construction is a part of writing that produces satisfying sentences.

18. Rules that fall under the heading of Parallel Writing are these:

    a. When naming _____, present them in the same way. Correct: "I was glad that I finished the project, attained my goal and received high commendation from my father." Incorrect: "I was glad that I finished the project, attained my goal and for receiving high commendation from my father."

    b. Place items in a _____ in similar locations. Correct: "When I feel sad, I often find myself walking, singing or praying." Incorrect: "When I feel sad, I often find myself on a walk, singing or sometimes I pray."

    c. Order items in a series by _____ or degree of importance. Correct: "I hope the man I marry loves the Lord, has a clear idea of calling and can make a good income." Incorrect: "I hope the man I marry can make a good income, has a clear idea of calling and loves the Lord."

    d. Use _____ for items in a series consistently and correctly. Correct: "He missed work last month on last Monday, on every Tuesday and on last Saturday." Incorrect: "He missed work last month on Monday, Saturday, and Tuesdays."

    e. Sentences constructed in a parallel way are often more _____. Give some examples.

    _____
    _____
    _____
    _____

19. _____ are used with contractions, possessive nouns, rare plural forms of some words and, often, are used incorrectly.

20. Make contractions of these words: is not, cannot, she will, you have, it is:

    _____
    _____

21. If a _____ noun does not end in an –s, its possessive form ends in –'s.

22. Make the necessary changes to correctly show possession with these word combinations using –'s:

    a. The hair belonging to Mercy _____

    b. The son belonging to Joey _____

    c. The cutting board owned by your mother _____

    d. The recipe that came from Emily _____

    e. The smile of the baby _____

23. Most plural nouns end in –s. To show possession, add an apostrophe _____ the final –s. List some examples.

    _____
    _____

24. Most singular words ending in –s form the possessive by adding –'s after the final –s, unless _____ considerations oppose this ending. In those cases, add the apostrophe after the final –s of the singular noun. List some examples.

    _____
    _____
    _____
    _____

25. Show possession correctly using the following sets of words:

    a. The harp belong to Miss Sims _____

    b. The railings of the bridges _____

    c. The tablets belonging to Moses _____

d. The disciples of Jesus _____

26. Apostrophes come in handy to help form _____ or provide _____ as in, "Don't add too many –s's to those words."

27. Give some examples of the statement above.

_____

_____

_____

_____

28. Apostrophes can be used to indicate _____ or quantity. "He gave two weeks' notice." "Give me two yards' worth of velvet." Note: The addition of the word "worth" makes "yards" possessive. If you wrote: "two yards of velvet," there would be no need for an apostrophe.

29. Apostrophes can be used to indicate the _____ of figures in dates. "The summer of '69 was the summer I got engaged."

30. Apostrophes are often used to indicate omission of _____ in informal writing or dialogue, as in, "We landed in Jo'berg when we flew into South Africa."

Writing Exercises

Exercise 1

Make a list of five people who would love to receive notes from you. On scrap paper, write a brief 1,2,3 outline of what you'd like to say to each one. Use your prettiest paper, note card or stationery, a nice pen with the color of ink you like best and your best penmanship to execute a note to each one. Be sure to check the address and correct spelling of names and addresses before you write in ink! Be sincere in what you write as well as brief.

Exercise 2

Write a three-paragraph paper describing the most embarrassing moment of your life (to date). Go back over it and make sure you have properly applied the rules for parallel expression. Correct your spelling, grammar and sentence construction and re-write it. Then, send it to me—I'd love to know all about it! Can you make me laugh? Write to **mrs.morecraft@gmail.com**.

Now do the same for the most blissful moment in your life thus far. Have fun!

Exercise 3

Continue to study the next section of Jill Bond's book *Writing to God's Glory*.

Exercise 4

Work on the next section of vocabulary words from Appendix E in this study guide. Be sure to follow the suggested approach to learning these words. Remember that studying etymology is critical to aggressive vocabulary expansion.

LESSON 5
Making Miso Soup— The Clearness of the Sentence, cont'd

"If the Divine Creator has taken pains to give us delicious and exquisite things to eat, the least we can do is prepare them well and serve them with ceremony." —Fernand Point, quoted in *A Return to Sunday Dinner,* by Russell Cronkhite

1. Clear expression of your thoughts in _____ words will make your writing a joy to write and read.

2. "When we write we live _____ _____, before the face of God. He is, as it were, reading over our shoulders." —RBM

3. "Whatever we do should be an _____ to _____, committed to Him for His glory." —RBM

4. True or false: Christians must always write about or mention Jesus, the Bible or God in their writing in order to write "Christianly." _____

5. When we attempt to write well, there's the problem of "_____"; that is, learning to be uniquely me when I write.

6. You have been given a gift that is very, very special: you are _____ _____ _____ _____. When God thought of you, He made you like no one else.

7. _____ is fine as long as it doesn't corrupt who you are in the expression of your thoughts.

8. But you must be _____ _____ as you write.

9. Some suggestions for improving your writing skills:

   a. Expand your working _____ and your reading _____.

   b. Make strides in applying the basic rules of _____ to your writing.

   c. Strive to _____ and _____ God in all you write and you will be blessed in immeasurable ways, both personally and as you become a blessing to those who read your writing.

10. One of the strongest influences on the English language came from the Celtic-speaking peoples of Britain. We call their combined language _____-_____.

11. Can you choose the correct word for each underlined portion in the sentences below?

    a. "Thank you for praying for Joe and <u>I (or me)</u>."

    b. "Everyone loves <u>their (or his)</u> mother."

    c. "Judy and <u>me (or I)</u> are leaving now."

    d. "They put all the blame on him and <u>me (or he and I)</u>."

e. "He jumped up <u>like (or as if)</u> he had a bee in his britches."

12. A good rule of thumb is to write for your _____.

13. In other words, if you are writing a children's book, choose words that are _____ and _____ to _____.

14. If you are writing a historical novel, make sure your words fit the _____ _____ about which you are writing.

15. I am not suggesting that you write to please _____ rather than God. To do so could lead to your lowering your standards in ways that are unbiblical.

16. Is it necessary to write lengthy, complicated sentences with stilted language in order to write intelligently? Why or why not?

_____

_____

_____

_____

17. The goal of your writing for the public should be to _____, _____, _____ and _____ your audience.

18. What is a split infinitive? Is it always wrong to split an infinitive? Give some examples of split infinitives and then correct them.

_____

_____

_____

_____

19. A good way to avoid splitting an infinitive is to _____ the word *to*. For instance, instead of writing "He helped me to finally find my seat," write instead, "He helped me finally find my seat." There!

20. _____ conjunctions can be remembered with the acronym FANBOYS. Do you remember what the initials stand for? How are these kinds of conjunctions used in a sentence? Write a sentence using this kind of conjunction correctly.

_____
_____
_____
_____

An additional set of conjunctions which were not discussed during this lecture but mentioned in another lecture are correlative conjunctions. They add another layer of connectivity between clauses. Here is the list:

both . . . and

not only . . . but also

either . . . or

neither . . . nor

whether . . . or

just as . . . so too

Write several sentences using these sets of conjunctions properly.

_____
_____
_____
_____
_____
_____

_____

_____

_____

21. _____ conjunctions establish the relationship between the dependent clause which they introduce and the rest of the sentence, subordinating the clause which they introduce to a place of lesser importance than the main or independent clause. Can you list some of these conjunctions? Write a sentence using this kind of conjunction correctly.

_____

_____

_____

_____

22. The problem that arises with subordinating conjunctions is that, while using them properly can strengthen a sentence, using them incorrectly can _____ it.

For instance:

"While writing is a good exercise, skipping rope is better." This sentence is confusing because the conjunction "while" is not the best choice here. *While* suggests two or more activities that occur simultaneously or consecutively. "While jogging through the park, I sprained my ankle."

An improved sentence that conveys more exactly what was intended in the first sentence would read:

"Although writing is a good exercise for brain cells, skipping rope is better for cardio health."

Be careful to use good logic with subordinating conjunctions and employ them to the best advantage in order to build strong sentences, not weaken them.

23. Let's review sentence structure. A _____ sentence gives us information contained in a complete thought, has a subject and a predicate (verb) and is an _____ clause that can stand alone.

24. A _____ is a single word or cluster of words that together work in your sentence as a single part of speech and cannot stand alone as a complete sentence.

25. Phrases come in five varieties. What are they?

_____
_____
_____
_____
_____

26. Can you label the various phrases mentioned above in this sentence?

    "Mrs. Morecraft sings an aria from an opera while she cleans the kitchen after dinner."

27. Each phrase completes the original thought—"Mrs. Morecraft sings"—and adds specific information for the reader. Try separating the information in this sentence and writing short sentences that give the same information to the reader.

28. Which type of sentence is more pleasing to read, the longer sentence or short ones that contain the same information? Why?

_____
_____
_____
_____
_____
_____

29. "Have you thought much about your future generations? Do you realize that even now at a very young age you are building a spiritual, mental and physical _____ to pass on to future generations?" —RBM

30. Here are some things that you as a young person can do to start building towards your future:

    a. Work to equip yourself to run an _____ household.

    b. Learn how to be an _____ homemaker.

    c. Learn how to be _____.

    d. Analyze and hone your God-given _____ and graces.

    e. Make wise use of _____.

31. _____ and _____–_____ are indispensable tools in our hands to help us shape our futures.

32. "A well-spoken, gracious young lady or young gentleman possesses a _____ to almost any circle, whether of common or royal rank."
    —RBM

33. Three goals to aim for as you study these webinar classes are these:

    a. How to _____ clearly, intelligently and with grace

    b. How to _____ with precision, logic and correctness

    c. How to be _____ and _____, a friend who acts with kindness and propriety and thinks of others first, adding a little _____ when appropriate.

34. Simply applying the rules of good grammar and sentence structure will not assure a writer that his writing is _____. Unless you write _____, you write in vain.

    a. One mistake commonly made is called _____ _____ which occurs when the subject and verb used don't make sense together. For instance, "His new car assured him of a ride to school every day." No, the car

149

can't assure him of anything. However, "Because he had a new car, he was assured of a ride to school every day," is a logical expression of thought.

b. _____ _____ occurs if you join (combine or coordinate) two clauses in an illogical way.

"I found my old roommate in the college phonebook and I almost gave it away." That's not very logical and quite an uncomfortable thought, actually. A better sentence would read: "I found my former roommate's phone number in the old college phonebook which I almost gave away."

c. Words that cannot be compared or qualified are called _____ _____. Finding examples of this misuse of words is a lot of fun. Here are a few: "The look on his face was nearly blank." Was it or wasn't it blank? "He was mostly dead from the piano that fell on him." Oh, dear. I fear one cannot be mostly dead. Can you list more words like the two in these sentences (dead and blank) that cannot be compared or qualified?

_____

_____

d. Never use _____ words (more, most, quite, rather, somewhat, very, etc.) in front of the words listed above or you will be considered mostly illogical.

35. _____ can be used in place of quotation marks to point out a character's thoughts. Here's an example:

"He had thought to find water over the next hill but the creek bed was a dust bowl. *I've heard that dying of thirst is a terrible way to go.* He tried to remember when he'd last seen water. *Was it two, no three days ago?* Panic began to set in. *I don't want to die like this!* He must find water. . ."

36. _____ are generally used to format titles of newspapers, movies, books, plays and other literary or artistic works. When you're mentioning shorter works or portions of works such as poems, articles, chapter titles and names of songs, use quotation marks.

37. _____ are frequently used to highlight a word or phrase so the reader isn't confused by your meaning. "Remember this trick for the correct

spelling of the word for paper used for letters, as opposed to the word meaning to stand still: the *e* in stationery stands for envelope, while the *a* in stationary stands for 'Attention!'"

Writing Exercises

Exercise 1

Look back over the notes and questions for this unit. Choose three writing errors that were discussed and write several sentences that show the faulty way to write (such as with split infinitives, weak and strong uses of subordinating conjunctions, etc.) and then rewrite them correctly.

Exercise 2

Go over the notes from this lecture on illogical sentences. Write several sentences illustrating each example and then correct them. Have fun!

Exercise 3

Continue with the instruction and assignments suggested by Jill Bond in her book *Writing to God's Glory*.

Exercise 4

Follow the instructions for the next set of words from the vocabulary lists in Appendix E.

LESSON 6
The Dessert Course: Choosing the Right Word—Delicious Diction

"We all have hometown appetites. Every other person is a bundle of longing for the simplicities of good taste once enjoyed on the farm or in the hometown left behind." —Clementine Paddleford, quoted in *A Return to Sunday Dinner* by Russell Cronkhite

1. Diction has to do with word _____. Good diction means choosing the right word that expresses exactly _____ _____ _____ _____ _____.

2. Why expand your vocabulary? It leads to an expansion of your _____.

3. "It is nearly impossible to be broadly and deeply educated without a _____ _____ on many levels of the vocabulary, or _____, of words from various fields and strata of learning." —RBM

4. "As you expand your reading and working vocabularies, that is, vocabularies that you can _____ but may not necessarily use in every day conversation or writing, you will find your ability to _____ logically and to _____ yourself concisely grow exponentially." —RBM

5. Two essential tools that are necessary for the task of vocabulary expansion are: a reliable _____ and a thesaurus. (I don't believe I got around to mentioning the second tool in the lecture. I got carried away talking about the first one.)

6. Mrs. Morecraft's favorite dictionary is _____ because of the Biblically sound content.

7. What three things stand out in your mind when you hear biographical information about Noah Webster?

_____

_____

_____

8. Remember when considering word choices that _____ conveys your meaning clearly.

9. The steps suggestions for writing are as follows:

   a. Decide what your topic will be and make a rough _____.

   b. Then, just write. If you have trouble beginning, try an exercise in _____.

   c. Here's how it's done: don't worry about spelling or _____.

   d. Don't worry about whether your ideas adhere or move in a _____ _____.

   e. Don't _____ anything yet.

   f. Don't be bothered that you _____-_____ from your topic.

g. Don't stop writing to look up _____; if you can't think of the word you're looking for, type -x's.

h. Do give yourself a 10-15 minute _____–_____ before you go back over what you've written and begin making deletions and corrections.

10. Another method to help you develop ideas or seed thoughts is to _____ _____ _____ like an interviewer.

11. In this method, pick any general topic and begin to _____ yourself, like a reporter.

    Ask these questions about your topic:

    a. _____ are the main characters in your story/poem/article/essay?

    b. _____ is the central theme of their actions?

    c. _____ does the action happen?

    d. _____ does it take place?

    e. _____ is the goal or purpose of the action achieved?

12. Unless you are writing simply as a hobby, remember to write for your _____.

13. Sometimes using a pre-writing technique called clustering or _____ can help connect your thoughts in a more logical sequence.

14. Before you begin to write, you must decide what _____ of writing you intend to do.

15. A variety of writing categories are available to you:

    a. _____ ,telling a story

    b. _____ , explaining or giving information

    c. _____ , providing a written picture of someone, place or thing

d. _____, giving data or some other type of information

e. _____, detailing your thoughts or emotions

f. _____, attempting to influence others to share your opinions

g. _____, examining material and explaining what you think about it

16. Remember that you can improve most non-fiction by using lots of _____ _____ or _____ _____.

17. "If you write a _____ statement before you begin to write and keep it where you can read it occasionally, you will be much better able to focus your thoughts as you write and keep to your subject with fewer rabbit trails."
—Susan Thurman, *The Only Grammar Book You'll Ever Need*, p. 136f

18. A _____ statement is a sentence of two stating what you intend to prove or what the central focus of your paper is about. It has been described as the mortar that holds the paper together.

19. More errors that occur when logic is not used in writing are these:

   a. _____ _____ will occur when you compare two unlike persons, places or things. "Weddings in June were more numerous than May." Comparing weddings and May is illogical because these two words are unlike. What was meant was this: "Weddings that took place in June were more numerous than those which took place in May."

   b. Writers who are in a hurry or who are lazy like to make _____ or _____ _____ which can lead to incorrect or exaggerated commentary. "Everyone booed the referee." "All his constituents joined in praise of our congressman's decision." "Nobody likes to see a grown man cry."

   c. In formal logic, a _____ _____ is an argument in which the conclusion does not follow from its premises. Therefore, the conclusion reached in such a fallacious argument can be either true or false. "I turned 21 yesterday; therefore, I am mature." Hmmm. . .maybe or maybe not. The premise is that attaining a certain age automatically makes one mature. Sorry, but this false premise will carry about as much water as a leaky bucket.

d. One frequent mistake in writing comes from _____ necessary words in comparisons which leads to illogical statements. "She told me her recipe was as good, if not better than Mom's." On the surface, this seems alright because we know what the writer meant to say, which was this: "She told me her recipe was as good as, if not better than, Mom's." Make sure when you write comparisons not to leave out simple words that "even up" the two phrases or clauses.

e. Another mistake is called in Latin _____ _____, _____ _____ _____, which translates *after this, so because of this*. The assumption is that because one thing follows another, the first caused the second. As an example: "Mercy washed her car in the morning, and it began to rain in the afternoon." The sentence structure implies that Mercy's washing of her car caused it to rain. Of course, this is illogical. A better way to write this would be: "Mercy washed her car in the morning and was sorry she had because it rained that afternoon."

f. A _____ _____ (sometimes called an either/or fallacy) states that only two alternatives exist, when there are actually more than two. "My dad said I could learn to wrestle or be a wimp."

g. A _____ _____ dodges the real issue by citing an irrelevant concern as evidence. "I pushed him because he looked like he was going to push me."

h. _____ _____ goes around in a circle with nothing substantial in the middle. "The little girl missed her dog because she was sad that he wasn't with her."

A word about legitimate circular reasoning is in order. Why do we believe that God's Word is holy, inspired and perfect? Because He says it is. Where do we find this information? In His holy and inspired Word. In the Bible, God reveals Himself as its Author and says it is trustworthy. We call this the _____-_____ nature of the Bible. There is no other book or revelation that makes these claims and proves itself true by the witness of the Holy Spirit in the hearts of His children. Therefore, although human reason is a gift of God and can and should be used to great benefit in our thinking, faith in the verity of God's witness about Himself and truthful testimony of His Word involves simple trust in Divine revelation rather than human reason. For the Christian, believing that God gave us a trustworthy witness about Himself and His creation in the Bible is quite reasonable and needs only to be embraced rather than "proved."

20. A _____ is a suspension of the voice in reading or speaking in order to make the meaning clearer or more impressive. There are two kinds of pauses: _____ pauses, introduced chiefly for the sake of clearness and indicated by punctuation marks; and _____ or rhetorical pauses in which the voice is paused or suspended for the purpose of rendering words or phrases more impressive or emphatic.

Writing Exercises

Exercise 1

Go back to our discussion of pre-writing techniques and try your hand at the mapping or the word association method. Think of something that interests you about which you'd like to write. Place that word or phrase in a circle in the middle of a blank piece of paper. Now think of other words or phrases that you associate with the first one and place them in smaller circles outside the bigger one with lines connecting them to the middle circle. As you write new words or phrases, others that are connected with the new ones will come to mind. Put them in circles that connect to the first layer of words. Keep doing this until you have no more words or room left. Read over the various circles you've created on the page. Do some fall together in your mind as a possible lead into a story or poem or essay? Try to choose a central theme and write a brief outline describing what you'd like to say. Write a thesis sentence, a sentence or two that states what you want to prove or write about. Now begin to write and draw in some of the words or ideas that are in the outer circles, if it seems logical. Don't stop to correct anything yet, just write. Give yourself a 15-minute time limit. Next, go back over what you've written and start eliminating any words, phrases or sentences that would improve the structure and rearrange the sequence of words or sentences, if necessary. Look for grammatical, punctuation and spelling errors last. Re-write and read your finished product to someone. Have fun!

Exercise 2

Write three sentences for each of these errors in writing involving logic: faulty comparisons, generalizations and *non sequiturs*. Write your sentences incorrectly first and then correct them.

Exercise 3

Continue with the next section of Jill Bond's book *Writing to God's Glory*.

Exercise 4

Look up and do the suggested exercises with the next set of vocabulary words from Appendix E.

LESSON 7
A Happy Ending to a Good Meal—the Fruit, Cheese & Chocolates

"Every meal should be a small celebration. If you acknowledge so joyous a fact of life, the pride you take in your efforts in the kitchen won't be confined to company occasions." —Marion Cunningham, quoted in *A Return to Sunday Dinner* by Russell Cronkhite

1. Some suggestions from the editors of the book we used in this course *100 Words Every High School Graduate Should Know*, for encouragement in expanding your vocabulary:

    a. Take your time—if ten words is too many, learn one or two new words a week. Not just the definitions but the _____ (history and connections), _____ and pronunciation and spelling. Try to use the words in conversation, even if you're just explaining it to a friend.

    b. If you already know the word we've listed, go to that page in your dictionary and _____ _____ _____ with which you aren't so familiar.

c. _____ back to your vocabulary list, refreshing your memory by reading through the definitions and other information you gleaned for each word. Test yourself to see if you remember how to use the word and its variations in sentences.

d. Keep your own ongoing vocabulary list in a _____ or on your _____. When you encounter an unfamiliar word while reading or in a sermon, lecture or any other resource, jot it down in your pocket notebook and then look it up later, going through the same process used for our vocabulary lists.

2. Common grammatical mistakes abound with English words. Our language is quite complicated, not only to someone learning it as a second or third language, but even to those who grew up speaking and writing it as a first language. Look at the sentences below and choose and circle the word or words in **bold letters** that illustrate correct usage. Can you explain your choices?

    a. "Joe and I are going for a walk. Would you like to come with **him and me / he and I**?"

    b. He doesn't believe that you're older than **I / me**.

    c. We may not be as rich as **them / they**, but I think we're a lot happier.

    d. "Does your toddler still **lie / lay** down for a nap?"

    e. I **could / couldn't** hardly believe my eyes when I saw what I'd been paid.

    f. You should **of / have** put more sugar in the lemonade.

    g. Julie feels that her **brothers-in-law / brother-in-laws** are more like brothers to her.

    h. What kind **of / of a** car are you looking for?

    i. She was delighted that **she / her** and John had been invited to the party.

    j. What **effect / affect** has the economy had on your family?

    k. Encouraging young writers has been one of the **principal / principle** goals of this webinar.

    l. I can't remember **who / whom** said that.

LESSON 7: A HAPPY ENDING TO A GOOD MEAL—THE FRUIT, CHEESE & CHOCOLATES

m. The baby **lay / laid** quietly, sucking his thumb.

n. No one but **she / her** made a perfect score.

o. Neither of your responses **are / is** satisfactory.

p. In the old days, horse thieves were **hung / hanged**.

q. Either of the cars **is / are** sure to catch your attention.

r. Tell **whoever / whomever** is waiting to come in.

s. We have found a young man **who / whom** we believe will work out fine for the job.

t. She's one of those writers who **turn / turns** out one popular novel after another.

u. I was completely **uninterested / disinterested** in the offer.

v. Use two **cupsful / cupfuls** of water in the recipe.

w. Do you mean to **infer / imply** that he's a liar?

x. We thought the writer to be **her / she**, but we were wrong.

y. Was it **she / her** you mentioned earlier?

z. **It's / Its** a sure thing that **its / it's** color isn't really red.

3. The following list of criteria was used to judge my writing contest. See if you can fill in the blanks with important missing words. These standards should prove helpful as you proof your writing.

    a. _____ accuracy

    b. strong, imaginative _____ that avoids tired, trite phrases, jargon or slang

    c. good _____ _____ and first paragraphs

    d. a clearly understood _____ of the _____

    e. a strong _____ paragraph

    f. good _____ _____ with strong nouns, verbs and properly used _____

163

g. for rhyming poetry, strict adherence to the chosen _____

h. for unrhymed poetry, strong, palpable _____ that is appropriate to the subject

i. skillful use of _____ _____ where applicable

j. _____ that capture interest for both poetry and prose

k. Did the writing grab and keep our interest throughout, or was the piece:

   i. too _____ (instructional with little to keep interest in a storyline)

   ii. too _____ (either too silly and unbelievable or impossible situations)

   iii. too _____ (yawn inspiring)

   iv. too _____ (trying to impress with big words, long, complicated sentences, etc.)

l. With article and essays, did the writer _____ and _____ a point well?

m. In all types of writing, did the writer _____ a _____ with us so that we wanted to keep reading and felt satisfied when we finished the piece? Were we either _____, _____, or for some reason made to feel glad we had read the piece?

4. Learning how to _____ the reader's _____, not through soupy, sentimental or stilted writing, but in a way that strikes a chord in the heart, is something more often _____ than learned. Ask God for this ability as you write.

5. Books that help expand your usable vocabulary, such a Norman Lewis' book *Word Power Made Easy*, are important assets to serious writers because of the new levels of knowledge they open up in _____, or the history of words, as well as _____ and _____, or word usage and choice.

6. Can you correctly match the list of common prefixes, suffixes and root words below with their meanings or uses?

   a. par   1. with, together

   b. –ment   2. negative prefix

   c. –ity   3. equal

   d. dis-   4. noun suffix attached to verbs

   e. con-, com-   5. noun suffix attached to adjectives

   f. vox, vocis   6. verb suffix

   g. –ate   7. both

   h. –ion   8. adjective suffix

   i. –ous   9. noun suffix attached to verb ending in –ate

   j. ambi-   10. voice

7. Mignon Foggarty informs us of the proper order of lists of modifiers in sentences in her book *The Grammar Devotional*. Please re-order the list below correctly according to Miss Foggarty's suggestions and write a sentence that illustrates this point, p. 190.

   a. size, b. opinion, c. age, d. color, e. shape, f. purpose, h. material, i. origin

   _____
   _____
   _____
   _____

8. When a number falls at the beginning of a sentence, most sources recommend _____ _____ the _____ rather than the _____.

9. But if the number is _____ _____, it's better to rewrite the sentence so that the number is in the middle.

10. The _____ _____ in verbs is usually discouraged; however, it's better to use it when writing out huge numbers than risk confusion.

11. When you aren't writing equations, the most common rule for writing numbers is to use _____ for the numbers one through nine and _____ for everything larger.

12. When dealing with statistics, use percent with a number and _____ without a number.

13. If you are using a percent—or any numeral—that's less than one, make sure you put a _____ before the decimal point.

14. When writing about time and money, think of the years, days, minutes or dollars as _____ the noun. That means the correct way to write such phrases is with an _____. _____ numbers are counting numbers: 1,2,3,4,5,6, etc. _____ numbers indicate the order of something: first, second, third, etc. In writing dates, only use _____ numbers before the name of the month.

15. Test your ability to discern between accepted current usage and dictionary meanings of the words listed below. Write a "D" above the dictionary definition and a "P" for the definition in popular usage today. When you write, be aware of both kinds of usage and choose your words according to the type of writing you are doing. If it's more formal writing, such as an essay or paper proving a technical point, the dictionary meaning is your safest reference point. If you are writing an article, story with dialogue or just for fun, the more popular usage would probably be acceptable. Use good judgment. (My reference here is Patricia O'Conner in *Woe is I*, p. 79f)

   a. **unique:** "one of a kind" or "unusual"?

   b. **decimate:** "to destroy one in ten" or "to destroy in part"?

   c. **diagnose:** "a doctor's evaluation of a disease" or "a doctor's evaluation of a patient"?

   d. **dilemma:** "a situation involving at least two choices, neither of them preferable" or "a difficult situation"?

e. **fun:** "a noun, a thing" or "an adjective describing a subject"?

f. **hopefully:** "an adverb meaning: in a hopeful manner" or "an adjective describing an attitude"?

16. Mrs. O'Conner lists several sets of words that are often confused by modern writers. Choose and circle the correct word in each of the sentences below. Be ready to defend your choice.

    a. "I never **accept/except** gifts from strangers."

    b. "She spoke to everyone in the room **accept/except** me."

    c. "These lessons have had a very positive **affect/effect** on my writing skills."

    d. "The desired **affect/effect** has been achieved, that of improved vocabulary and more grammatically correct sentences."

    e. "Scratching **aggravates/irritates** the itch."

    f. "Those who use incorrect grammar in public ads and television programs **aggravate/irritate** me exceedingly."

    g. "Miss Elizabeth Bennett sensed a barrier **between/among** her and Mr. Darcy."

    h. "Darcy's arrival created a stir **between/among** the guests."

    i. "**Regretfully/Regrettably**, I must close these study guides in just a few minutes."

    j. "**Regretfully/Regrettably**, because of distance, I cannot visit each of my students personally, but I can still pray for each of them."

17. As we speak or sing, our voices will change pitch or _____ from one pitch to another. As you carefully consider how to _____ the tone and pitch of your voice, you will find it a very flexible instrument that you can train to achieve a more pleasing sound.

18. _____ in our speech are as diversified as the emotions behind them.

19. Learning to control the _____ of your voice, whether you are singing, reading aloud or simply carrying on a conversation, will make your speaking voice more agreeable and a pleasure to your listeners.

Writing Exercises

Exercise 1

As we studied Norman Lewis' book *Word Power Made Easy*, we discovered secrets of etymology that enable us to explore whole families of words as we connect them to their root words, prefixes or suffixes. Choose from one of these words, prefixes or suffixes below and write several sentences, or even a three-paragraph essay or article, using a many words as you can from the connected word-family of the root words, prefixes or suffixes you choose.

par, dis-, equ- or aequus, -ment, -ity, con-, com-, vox or vocis, -ate, -ion, -ous, ambi-

Exercise 2

Go back to the first lesson in which you participated. Pull out the first article/essay, poem or group of sentences you wrote. Compare them to what you are writing now. Do you see improvement? Describe in three paragraphs what you feel you have learned or gained from taking these classes. Send your responses to me, if you'd like (**mrs.morecraft@gmail.com**). I love hearing from you. Don't forget to check my blog occasionally for updates and musings: **becky-gracenotes.blogspot.com**.

Exercise 3

Continue studying Jill Bond's book *Writing to God's Glory* to its completion.

Exercise 4: Vocabulary and Word Studies

Follow the instructions at the beginning of the vocabulary lists in Appendix E and continue through them at your own pace until you have reached their conclusion. Remember the added advice of choosing another word from the dictionary with which you are less familiar if you come across one on the list that has already been added.

Volume I
Answer Key

ANSWER KEY—LESSON 1
Foundational Principles for Christian Writers

1. The paragraph should include a reference to developing our writing and speaking skills for some of these worthy goals: developing a Christian mindset, developing a Christian worldview, developing a Christian conscience, developing the desire for excellence, developing a heart to do all for the glory of God. Although mentioned elsewhere in these lectures, personal development, informing and delighting our readers and listeners are also important goals.

2. Charlemagne enjoyed hearing selections from St. Augustine's *City of God* read to him.

3. Queen Elizabeth I

4. Abigail Adams to her husband John Adams in 1776

5. A metaphor is figurative language that compares one thing to another without using *like* or *as*; a simile is a figure of speech that uses *like* or *as* in making comparisons.

6. "workmanship" The literal translation from the Greek is "poem"

7. Reference from the lecture: "God thinks of me as a beautifully constructed

"poem." He is obviously not finished constructing! Some days, I sense Him moving around some of the verbs (those actions I do or don't accomplish) to make me (His poem) stronger. I have seen many of the "nouns"—things, people, places—moved about, some completely deleted, like when my house burned down several years ago and most of the things I thought I couldn't live without were gone. He is always about tweaking His poem, me, making me more beautiful in His sight. I like that thought! This should inspire you in your writing as well, since we are to love the things God loves. He obviously loves His people who are His poems ... we should love to create beautiful sentences and imagery as well." —RBM

Reference from the lecture: "Writing records a piece of history that is unique to you. You are a conglomeration of genes, characteristics, talents and all the rest, born at the exact moment in history that God chose for you before the foundations of the world were laid. There may be others who look like you or have the same accent or wear similar clothing. But you are unique–there is no one with your exact DNA or fingerprints or spark of life like the ones He chose just to make you YOU!" —RBM

8. writing

9. "...so is he."

10. beliefs, inmost thoughts

11. self, God; God, self.   John Calvin in his *Institutes of the Christian Religion*, I.i. & I.ii.

12. from the lecture: "Keep a brief record of how God has blessed you in some way, the struggles and successes you encounter from day to day, a prayer journal, funny things children say and do ... Journaling is an important way to grow in grace, to mature as you grow, to recount God's blessing in the midst of your struggles; and for young children and even older ones, it's great writing practice. ... [Journal] so that your great-grandchildren will be able to see what you were thinking. Well, there's another reason to be careful what we write." RBM

13. "As you develop characters and plot, have a definite point from which you begin and have a specific goal to which you are going. Wind it around in as many ways as your sanctified imagination takes you, skillfully, of course, but prove your point! Therein lies the pathway to a good paper, article, story, or book." RBM

14. type, style or genre–either word or concept is correct in this sentence

15. evil

16. extolling the virtues of King Jesus in every sphere of life
17. how beautiful the universe really is
18. redemption, providence
19. journals, blogs, stories, historical narrative, journalism, screenplays, movies, poetry, articles, songs
20. The essay should include some of these ideas along with their own ideas: Knowing what the Bible teaches helps me "think God's thoughts" after Him and gives a grid through which to sift my ideas so that what I write will be in conformity to the truth about life that I find in His Word.
21. thinks like he thinks
22. glory, build up, edify, encourage
23. *coram Deo*
24. fact, fiction
25. morally
26. the Bible, the Westminster Confession of Faith and Larger and Shorter Catechisms
27. exactly what you put into it, grace
28. industrious, industrious
29. b., the Word of God
30. **denotation**: the most specific or literal meaning of a word as opposed to its figurative senses; **connotation**: the implying or suggesting of an additional meaning for a word or phrase apart from the literal or main meaning.

ANSWER KEY—LESSON 2
Laying a Firm Foundation—Good Grammar & Her Friends

1. list key words, leave room for other important words connected to key words, go back later to fill in the gaps, abbreviate, develop your own shorthand or learn standard proofreading shorthand notation, sketch or illustrate the subject matter, keep notes in a journal for future reference.

2. nouns, verbs, modifiers

3. simple elegance

4. detective

5. change verb tenses

6. three tenses are present, past and future. Various forms are progressive, perfect and perfect progressive. Examples: present—I bake, I am baking, I have baked or have been baking.

7. Present, acknowledged fact

ANSWER KEY—LESSON 2

8. a–ii, b–iii, c–i

9. started, finished

10. –ed, irregular

11. could be various verbs

12. mix

13. true

14. vignette

15. snapshot or photo, camera, development

16. How do I want to write about it (the photo)? Which genre will I choose—a poem, story, song, play? What are some word choices? Which ones best fit the action? What emotions do I want to convey?

17. mystery

18. experiences

19. read aloud practice

20. you must learn quiet

21. listen, look and jot down what you see and hear; jot down everyday experiences and write about them later; think deeply and broadly about what you are experiencing; keep a notepad handy to jot down ideas; keep a journal; learn to focus your thoughts on Christ.

22. true

23. accepted literary standards

24. create quiet; listen to the experts; use research materials; expand your vocabulary and explore words; improve your spelling techniques; read good books; read what you write aloud to someone for their input; don't be afraid of criticism and learn to re-write.

25. read a portion of a well-written book and examine how it is written, then just copy it on paper or try your hand at writing something similar.

26. deserted

ANSWER KEY—LESSON 3
Poetry: Harbinger of Hope & Glimmers of Glory

1. *ex nihilo*

2. false, He created the universe and all it contains to reflect His glory

3. the Word

4. rational, deeper meaning

5. complex patterns, complex

6. emotions, elevated thoughts, intimate scenes

7. Bible

8. metaphor: The Lord is my shepherd; I am the vine you are the branches; in the beginning was the word and the word was with God and the word was God; —Job 38:4f...

9. simile: He shall be like a tree.... —Psalm 1, 3, 4

10. clear, powerful; sensory, palpable

11. powerful feelings, emotion

12. few words; exact language; minute visual, auditory and sensory descriptions; memories of real-life experiences.

13. **personification:** words depicting non-human things or ideas as if they were human—"a sweating sword."
    an apostrophe: the poem's narrator addresses an inanimate object or abstraction as if it were present and alive: "O death, where is thy sting?"
    hyperbole: also called overstatement, can be used to express strong feeling such as, "all night I made my bed to swim with my tears..."
    understatement: saying less to say more: "The grave's a fine, quiet place..."
    metaphor: figurative language that compares one thing to another without using "like" or "as."
    simile: a figure of speech that uses "like" or "as" in making comparisons.

14. express the inexpressible

15. literary devices

16. place, like, as

17. the Word, the Bread of Life, the Water of Life, the Resurrection and the Life, the Door, the Way, the Vine, the Lamb of God, the good Shepherd

18. "Like a gold ring in a pig's snout, so is a lovely woman who lacks discretion." —Proverbs 11:22 (a simile); "Wisdom crieth...she uttereth her voice...," —Proverbs 1:20f (metaphor); "A wholesome tongue is a tree of life...." — Proverbs 15:4 (metaphor).

19. plural, singular

20. subject-verb

21. various

22. above, about, across, against, along, among, around, at, etc.

23. preposition

24. your meaning is clear without them

25. preposition

26. awkward, a.

27. various

28. read aloud

29. change the minds

30. have a clear objective, maintain unfaltering focus, present compelling alternative to the status quo, master all the devices and protocols of art and story.

ANSWER KEY—LESSON 4
Gathering & Planting

1. word gatherer

2. 1-c, 2-a, 3-b, 4-d

3. Anglo-Saxon, Anglo-Saxon

4. precision, few modifiers

5. directness, brevity, plainness

6. William Shakespeare

7. various

8. clichés

9. genre

10. strong, concise

11. blank verse

12. a thousand words

13. good poetry—strong nouns and verbs, sensory, compact imagery, expression of emotion without instructing the reader how to react; poor poetry—vague

nouns and weak verbs, too many modifiers, trite imagery, contrived rhyming patterns

14. yourself, naturally, plan

15. read good books

16. nouns, verbs

17. adjective

18. toughness, color

19. toughness, color, reading vocabulary, storehouse, storehouse

20. (a.) energy source, modifiers, dullness (b.) precise, look—gaze, stare, peer, peek, gawk, etc.; throw—hurl, flip, toss, ratchet, etc.; eat—wolf it down, gobble it up, slurp, graze, shovel it in, etc.; give—gift, present, award, deliver, pass, grant, convey, impart, provide, etc.(c.) active (d.) passive

21. word

22. connotations

23. modifiers

24. adjectives

25. adverbs, adverb

26. false

27. tangledly, tiredly, sweepingly, etc.

28. various

29. revise and rewrite

30. wordiness

31. excess

32. qualifiers

33. examples are rather, very, little, pretty, usually, about

34. spontaneity–look it up!

35. write in a way that is compact, informative and unpretentious...also, keep a tight

    rein on the material and stay out of "the act"

36. if you don't use a word in real conversation, don't use it when you write dialogue

37. aloud

38. pretentious, coy, cute; twenty-dollar, fancy, atrocious, felicitous

39. break the rules of grammar; ear, ear

40. clarity, muddiness

41. opinion, opinion

42. figures, speech

43. clarity

44. foreign languages

45. slang, jargon

46. cliches

47. sound bites

48. attitudes, principles, composition

49. thinks

ANSWER KEY—LESSON 5

Where Shall I Begin? A Few Novel Ideas for Story Starters

1. discussion

2. the first sentence snags the reader's attention

3. lead

4. within and around

5. look, through a writer's eyes

6. ordinary, lenses, ordinary, extraordinary

7. metaphor

8. review and rewrite

9. good grammar, punctuation, spelling, strong verbs and nouns, well-used modifiers, have a goal, begin with a strong lead, prove your point, conclude well

10. a strong character, an interesting incident, a spiritual characteristic that can be

personified in a story

11. stories

12. match

13. hint

14. reinforce

15. pivotal

16. climax

17. supporting role

18. suspense

19. narrative, anecdotes

20. anecdote, anecdotes

21. storyteller

22. what happens next, surprise, unexpected

23. delight, inspire

24. strong, dolphin, begin well and surprise and delight your reading with the telling of the tale, especially the ending

25. delight, wisdom, wisdom, delight

ANSWER KEY—LESSON 6
Journaling, Letter-Writing & E-mails—the Real You Showing Through

1. pleasurable discipline

2. an English naval administrator and member of Parliament

3. a. write; penmanship; composing interesting sentences;
   b. spark ideas;
   c. Clarify;
   d. track answers;
   e. your own history

4. His hand

5. living life

6. the weather; your surroundings; people; trips; work

7. The day is done and you can set down the happenings of the day and your reactions to them with more clarity and completion.

8. in order to sort out the experiences of the day so they don't run together in a blur; keeping a notebook at hand in order to jot down interesting or important events as they happen, quotes, comments, or sketches

9. Keep a notebook or diary/journal from day to day with the date at the top and activities, reactions, prayers and other ideas flowing from this.

10. journals are often made public later on – use caution in what you say

11. nouns

12. name

13. clear, concise, sense of reality

14. Personal

15. Possessive

16. Reflexive

17. Relative

18. subordinate

19. ex.: "Mary is the girl who first introduced me to the writings of Lucy Maud Montgomery."

20. parallelism

21. asking a question

22. antecedents

23. the word that came before

24. clause; scramble; he or him for who or whom

25. categorize

26. sight, smell, touch, taste, hearing – the appearance of uniforms, the way the soccer field looks, the enthusiasm of the crowd, the sounds of the ball being kicked or bounced off a head, players' faces, reactions to a goal, the smell of the air, etc.

27. details

28. specific, imagery, dialogue, notes

29. blank spaces

30. proper

31. addresses and ZIP codes

32. postage stamps

33. date

34. Address the envelope before writing the letter, stamp it and put your name and the return address in the upper left hand corner or on the back flap of the envelope. Now, you can take your time writing the letter, knowing that the mailing details are taken care of.

35. salutation; closing

36. body or text

37. post script

38. whom, why

39. communicate

40. beautiful script; writing paper; writing tools; scenting your writing papers; good posture.

41. style

42. best

43. hand-written letters

44. character, habits

ANSWER KEY—LESSON 7
Digging Deeper—Common Writing Errors

1. denotation, connotation

2. slang, colloquialisms, or jargon

3. because it distracts the reader

4. the correct answer is (a.) "to increase," as in, "His impression that she was a snob was aggravated by her disdainful glances at his worn shoes," rather than this incorrect usage: "He was aggravated by her disdainful glances."

5. only in dialogue where it makes sense

6. Apply *among* to more than two persons or things; use *between* with only two.

7. idioms

8. Best: "Her pies are as good as mine, or even better." An acceptable but weaker sentence would read: "Her pies are as good as or even better than mine."

9. redundant

10. very much—"I miss you very much."

11. rear, bring up

12. loose sentences

13. triteness, emptiness, mechanical symmetry becomes "sing-song-y"

14. "... recast enough of them to remove the monotony, replacing them by simple sentences or sentences of two clauses joined by a semi-colon or periodic sentences of two clauses, or by sentences, loose or periodic, of three clauses–whichever best represent the real relations of the thought."
—Strunk and White, *The Elements of Style*, p. 26

15. periodic

16. loose

17. maintain

18. "He maintained that the law upheld his rights."

19. active

20. sap

21. short, long

22. strong, precise

23. verbs

24. active, preposition

25. "Break it up into two short sentences or use a semi-colon or restructure it to make sure you are expressing a cogent thought from beginning to end." Zinsser, p. 68

26. exclamation points

27. punctuation

28. shift gears

29. but, and yet, however, nevertheless, still, instead, thus, therefore, meanwhile, now, later, today, yesterday, tomorrow, last night, this morning, subsequently, on the other hand, rather...

30. mood changers

31. orient

32. subjective

33. objective

34. various

35. cacophony

36. consonants

37. euphony

38. vowels

39. onomatopoeia

40. assonance

41. consonance, sound

42. alliteration, recitation

43. rhyme

44. exact rhyme

45. end rhyme

46. internal rhyme

47. freshness, cliché

48. forces poets to use certain words that may not be the most suitable for the poem's purpose

Volume II
Answer Key

ANSWER KEY—LESSON 1
The Soup Course—Grammar Served Up with a Sprig of Parsley

1. deconstruct

2. instruments or tools

3. words

4. nourishing and palatable (or similar adjectives)

5. Bread

6. pizzazz

7. God created an amazing array of species and within each a fascinating assortment of colors, types and variations. We can follow His cue in our food preparation by using a wide assortment of foods and in writing with careful, colorful combinations of words and topics, skillfully put together to provide both nourishment and delight.

8. sentence

ANSWER KEY—LESSON 1

9. subject

10. subject

11. noun, noun. pronoun

12. predicate

13. verb, verb

14. a. declarative

   b. interrogative

   c. imperative

   d. exclamatory

15. understood

16. whatever

17. modifiers

18. modifiers

19. adjectives

20. adverbs

21. complete subject

22. complete predicate

23. nouns–Joe, minister; Geneva, home; ladle, harness; happiness, Christianity

24. Common. Such as: person, city, country, man, church or store

25. Proper. Such as: Mr. Phillips, Atlanta, Italy, John Adams or Vision Forum Catalog

26. Collective common. Such as: army, committee, company or family

27. Collective proper. Such as: United States Army, the House Committee on Foreign Relations, Vision Forum Ministries or the Morecrafts

28. subject; direct object; indirect object; object of a preposition; predicate noun (or nominative); appositive; in direct address.

29. a. number

    b. gender

    c. person

    d. i. nominative case

       ii. objective case

       iii. possessive case

30. –s

31. -s, -z, -x, -sh, -ch, -ss

32. quiz–quizzes, Liz–Lizzes (more than one Liz), etc.

33. Because a pronounced –s begins with the vowel sound –eh, as in egg, thus we use *an* rather than *a* before it.

34. reference lecture or slideshow notes

35. conjunction, a. coordinating conjunctions, b. correlative, c. subordinating conjunctions

36. interjection

37. rhythm, direction, pitch, tone and flow

38. and, or

39. Oxford

40. places a comma after the final word in a series, before the *and* or *or*

41. "I love the old red, white, and blue flag."

42. be consistent

43. comma splice, run-on sentence

44. "I left my hat out in the rain, and when I returned, it was a soggy mess." "Because I left my hat out in the rain, when I returned, it was a soggy mess." or, "I left my hat out in the rain. When I returned, it was a soggy mess."

45. enclose

46. good reason

ANSWER KEY—LESSON 2
The Appetizer Course— Speaking & Writing with Agility & Grace

1. sentence

2. interest, long and short, interesting, accurate, imagery

3. a. long, b. choppy, c. incorrect, d. boring, e. impress, f. "fluff", g. repetitious, h. misspelled words, i. captivating, j. slang, k. inaccurate, l. information, m. audience

4. interests

5. subordinating conjunctions

6. vague, specific

7. tangible, ambiguous

8. Relative

9. relative clauses

10. emotion, greatness, right thinking, action, heart palpitations
11. damaging their reputations
12. subject-verb
13. time
14. intervening information
15. compound subject
16. singular, plural
17. a group of things–couple, total, majority, number
18. what
19. there, there, phantom
20. there
21. were, subjunctive
22. end stop
23. no
24. yes, to show that the sentence is over
25. don't
26. don't
27. various
28. Adverbial
29. subordinating conjunctions, conjunctions

ANSWER KEY—LESSON 3
The Salad Course— Tossing Together Clear Thinking with Clean Writing
(or how to clearly state your thoughts without overdoing the dressing)

1. stay away from what you've written for a few days

2. typos and misspelled words; grammatical errors; punctuation errors; does the style match the theme; word choice; clear meaning; keeping interest; reaching the goal of why you wrote it

3. sentence, sentence

4. subject (noun, pronoun or construction acting as a noun or pronoun), predicate (verb or construction acting as a verb)

5. related

6. phrase

7. clause

8. independent

9. dependent

10. ear

11. Who's coming? What recipe will I use? Do I have the necessary ingredients? Do I understand the basic instructions for combining them? Is there more than one way to make the recipe "work"? (For instance, could I substitute ingredients?) Would I change anything to make this recipe more delectable?

12. Who's my intended audience? What style should I use? Do I understand the elements necessary to write well in this particular style? What do I need to "brush up on" in order to sharpen my writing in this style? Can I change anything I've written to make it sound more like "me"? After reading what I've written, are there ingredients I could change to make my message more appealing or convincing?

13. a phrase or clause that is properly capitalized and punctuated as a sentence but does not express a complete thought

14. comma; "Soon after the bear ate her." (fragment) "Soon after, the bear ate her." (an introductory adverbial phrase, "soon after," separated by a comma, followed by an independent clause, "the bear ate her")

15. a. emphasis

    b. dialogue

    c. exclamations and interjections

16. a. A

    b. NA

    c. A

    d. NA

    e. A

    f. NA

    g. A

    h. A

THE SALAD COURSE—TOSSING TOGETHER CLEAR THINKING WITH CLEAN WRITING

 i. A

 j. NA

 k. NA

 l. NA

 m. NA

 n. NA

 o. A

 p. A

17. question marks

18. exclamation points

19. exclamation points

20. Anglo-Saxon

21. clear, pointed

22. a. you want to say

 b. say it

 c. your own language

 d. short word is better than a long one

23. fit for talk

24. living or dead

25. plagiarism

26. quotation marks

27. direct: "Give me the money, please," she said.

28. Indirect: She told me to give her the money.

29. direct dialogue: "Oh, yeah?" "Yeah."

30. end

31. beginning, start, closing

32. poems, stories, articles, essays, books, songs, episodes

33. slang, terminology, quotation marks

34. periods, commas, colons, semicolons

35. question marks, exclamation points

36. inside: "Did you fall asleep?"

37. outside: Did Martha say, "You must have fallen asleep"?

38. exclamation points

39. single

40. sentences

41. stress

42. pronunciation

43. loudness, softness

44. musical

45. stress

46. single sounds

47. initial, median, final

48. clichés

ANSWER KEY—LESSON 4
The Main Course—Writing a Sentence that Satisfies

1. have a plan
2. gratitude
3. "Dear"
4. better equipped, understood the times
5. a. reading comprehension, concepts;
   b. express yourself, precise, cogent;
   c. connections, imagery, etymology
6. etymology
7. root, root
8. root, root

9. etymological

ANSWER KEY—LESSON 4

- a. prefixes, suffixes
- b. structure
- c. construct
- d. verbs, verbs, nouns

10. etymology
11. modifiers
12. limiting
13. dangling
14. squinting
15. parallel
16. parallel
17. parallel
18.
    - a. items
    - b. series
    - c. chronology
    - d. prepositions
    - e. effective
19. apostrophes
20. isn't, can't, she'll, you've, he's, it's
21. singular
22.
    - a. Mercy's hair
    - b. Joey's son
    - c. Mom's cutting board
    - d. Emily's recipe
    - e. baby's smile
23. after

24. pronunciation

25. a. Miss Sims' harp

    b. the bridges' railings

    c. Moses' tablets

    d. Jesus' disciples

26. plurals, clarity

27. abbreviations with more than one period—M.D.'s, Ph.D.'s, etc.; proverbial expressions that involve individual letters or combinations of letters–mind your "p's and q's"

28. time

29. omission

30. letters

ANSWER KEY—LESSON 5
Making Miso Soup—The Clearness of the Sentence, cont'd

1. exact

2. *coram Deo*

3. offering, Jehovah

4. false

5. "voice"

6. one of a kind

7. imitation

8. correctly unique

9. a. vocabulary, vocabulary

   b. vocabulary

c. honor and glorify

10. Anglo-Saxon

11. a. "for Joe and me" because this construction acts as the object of the preposition "for"; therefore, "me" which is an objective case pronoun is used rather than "I" which is in the subjective case and acts as a subject rather than an object.

   b. "His mother" is correct because the subject of the sentence, "Everyone" is singular, not plural.

   c. "Judy and "I" because "I" is used as a subject rather than "me" which is in the objective case.

   d. "Him and me" is correct because both words are objective case pronouns, objects of the preposition "on."

   e. "As if" is correct since "like" has a different meaning (although if you are using this in dialogue, it would be acceptable since it is a commonly misused phrase today).

12. reader

13. appealing, easy to grasp

14. time period

15. man

16. No. In fact, that kind of writing will probably lose an audience very quickly. Write simply and clearly, not in an effort to impress.

17. delight, surprise, inform, move

18. A split infinitive occurs when a word is inserted between the word to and the verb: to eventually succeed (to succeed eventually); to completely fail (to fail completely). The judges are still out on the right or wrongness of splitting an infinitive. However, if splitting the infinitive makes your sentence stronger, go ahead and split it. Remember, however, that in formal writing split infinitives are not acceptable, as a rule.

19. omit

20. coordinating; for, and, nor, but, or, yet, so; to connect two independent clauses;

    "Jan and Mark wanted a boy, but they were just as happy when God gave them a girl."

21. subordinating; after, although, as, because, before, if, since, than, though, unless, until, when, while

    "While January is a frosty, frozen time of year, March is always a-bloom in Georgia."

22. weaken

23. declarative, independent

24. phrase

25. noun, verb, adverb, adjective, prepositional

26. Mrs. Morecraft (noun phrase) sings (verb phrase) an aria (a noun phrase and direct object of the verb "sings") from an opera (a prepositional phrase acting as an adjective modifying "aria") while she cleans the kitchen (an adverbial phrase begun with the subordinating conjunction "while" and acting as an adverb) after dinner (a prepositional phrase acting as an adverb modifying "sings").

27. Mrs. Morecraft sings. She sings an aria. The aria is from an opera. She cleans the kitchen. She cleans the kitchen when dinner is finished.

28. The longer sentence that employs connecting words is more pleasing to read because the thoughts flow together.

29. Legacy

30. a. entrepreneurial

    b. efficient

    c. productive

    d. gifts

    e. time

31. Language, self-expression

32. passport

33. think, speak, winsome, gracious, humor

34. logical, logically

    a. faulty predication

    b. faulty coordination

c. absolute adjectives; complete, empty, eternal, favorite, permanent, pure, round, square, straight, true, unanimous, unique, vacant, dead, blank

  d. qualifying

35. Italics

36. Italics

37. Italics

ANSWER KEY—LESSON 6
The Dessert Course: Choosing the Right Word—Delicious Diction

1. choice; what you mean to say
2. thinking
3. working knowledge, lexicon
4. comprehend, analyze, express
5. dictionary
6. Webster's 1828 *An American Dictionary of the English Language*
7. various
8. exactness;

9. a. outline

   b. freewriting

   c. punctuation

   d. logical sequence

   e. correct

   f. rabbit-trail

   g. words

   h. time-limit

10. ask yourself questions

11. interview

    a. who

    b. what

    c. when

    d. where

    e. how

12. audience

13. mapping

14. type

15. a. narrative

    b. expository

    c. descriptive

    d. informative or explanatory

    e. expressive

    f. persuasive or argumentative

    g. analytical

16. specific examples, supporting details

17. thesis

18. thesis

19. a. faulty comparisons

    b. sweeping or hasty generalizations

    c. non sequitur

    d. omitting

    e. post hoc, ergo propter hoc

    f. a false dilemma

    g. a red herring

    h. circular reasoning; self-authenticating

20. pause; grammatical, elocutionary

ANSWER KEY—LESSON 7
A Happy Ending to a Good Meal—the Fruit, Cheese & Chocolates

1. a. etymology, usages
   b. choose another word
   c. Refer
   d. notebook, computer
2. a. him and me
   b. me
   c. they,
   d. lie
   e. could
   f. have

g. brothers-in-law
h. of
i. she
j. effect
k. principal
l. who
m. lay
n. her
o. is
p. hanged
q. is
r. whoever
s. who
t. turns
u. uninterested
v. cupfuls
w. imply
x. her
y. she
z. it's, its

3. a. grammatical
   b. imagery
   c. lead sentences
   d. development of the theme
   e. concluding
   f. sentence structure, modifiers

    g. meter

    h. imagery

    i. internal rhyme

    j. themes

    k. rhetorical, artificial, boring, wordy

    l. make, prove

    m. strike a chord, entertained, inspired

4. move, emotions, given

5. etymology, grammar, diction

6.
    a. 3

    b. 4

    c. 5

    d. 2

    e. 1

    f. 10

    g. 6

    h. 9

    i. 8

    j. 7

7. opinion, size, age, shape, color, origin, material, purpose

    "Mercy's beautiful, big, new, oblong, red, American-made, metal mixing machine was her favorite gift."

    "My son's ridiculously big, yellow, down-filled vest makes him truly visible."

    "I want to hike in the gorgeous, steep, Appalachian mountains this summer."

8. writing out, words, numerals

9. extremely long

10. passive voice

11. words, numerals

12. percentage

13. zero

14. owning, apostrophe, cardinal, ordinal, ordinal

15. In each example, the first definition is the more classical "dictionary" meaning of the word while the second definition is accepted modern usage.

16. a. accept

    b. except

    c. affect

    d. effect

    e. aggravates

    f. irritates

    g. between

    h. among

    i. Regretfully

    j. Regrettably

17. modulate, modulate

18. Inflections

19. Nuances

APPENDIX A
Poems, Quotations & Other Interesting Tid-bits

(**Note:** Citations of the resources quoted in this section and throughout the study guides may be found in the Sources & Resources section, Appendix B.)

1. In his exposition of Romans 8:28, *The Divine Cordial*, the Puritan pastor, Thomas Watson remarks: "There are two things, which I have always looked upon as difficult. The one is, to make the wicked sad; the other is, to make the godly joyful."

2. From "Ulysses" by Alfred, Lord Tennyson

   I cannot rest from travel: I will drink
   Life to the lees: all times I have enjoyed
   Greatly, have suffered greatly, both with those
   That loved me, and alone; on shore, and when
   Through scudding drifts the rainy Hyades
   Vexed the dim sea: I am become a name;
   For always roaming with a hungry heart

Much have I seen and known; cities of men
   And manners, climates, councils, governments,
   Myself not least, but honoured of them all;
   And drunk delight of battle with my peers;
   Far on the ringing plains of windy Troy.
   I am a part of all that I have met;
   Yet all experience is an arch wherethrough
   Gleams that untraveled world, whose margin fades
   Forever and forever when I move.
   How dull it is to pause, to make an end,
   To rust unburnished, not to shine in use!

3. From "Roots & Vines," by Rebecca B. Morecraft
   (for my mother)

   "Give her the fruit of her hands; let her own works praise her in the gates."
   —Proverbs 31:31

   My mother's roots wrap mine in pithy strength,
   fending off the August drought and creeping blight,
   the canker worms who fear her light and
   crawl back to their hollow darkness, cowering.
   Her blue eyes see clear down, through all my muddiness,
   to clumps that clog my springs of joy;
   and on her knees, with both hands tugging,
   she sees it right again.

   With hands outstretched, scattering seeds,
   she feeds us full to overflowing.
   No friend nor stranger passes by her door
   with needs denied.
   Her briars kept clipped, she harms not beast nor bird,
   but, ever abiding, props the weaker limbs
   with grace, distilling healing dew
   at pruning time.

4. "Without knowledge of self there is no knowledge of God . . . Without knowledge of God there is no knowledge of self."
   —John Calvin, *Institutes*, I.i. & I.ii.

5. "I was obliged to be industrious; whoever is equally industrious will succeed equally well." —J. S. Bach

6. "Farther Along"
    (a mountain song)

    Tempted and tried we're oft made to wonder
    Why it should be thus all the day long
    While there are others living around us
    Never molested, though in the wrong.

    Chorus:
    Farther along we'll know all about it;
    Father along we'll understand why.
    Cheer up, my brother, live in the sunshine.
    We'll understand it all by and by.

    When I see Jesus coming from glory,
    When He comes from His home in the sky,
    Then I shall join Him on that glad morning.
    We'll understand it all by and by.

    (repeat chorus)

7. "Who can confidently say what ignites a certain combination of words, causing them to explode in the mind? Who knows why certain notes in music are capable of stirring the listener deeply, though the same notes slightly rearranged are impotent? These are high mysteries . . . There is no satisfactory explanation of style, no infallible guide to good writing, no assurance that a person who thinks clearly will be able to write clearly, no key that unlocks the door, no inflexible rule by which writers may shape their course. Writers will often find themselves steering by stars that are disturbingly in motion." William Strunk, *Elements of Style*, by Strunk and White, 4th ed., p. 6.

8. "Briary Branch"
"...the branch cannot bear fruit of itself, unless it abide in the vine..."
—John 15:4

A briary branch extended
from rough and gnarly roots,
I see myself in these raspberry vines
as I transplant them from my Granny's patch.
My mother guarded well the gate and
with my father kept the ground
where these vines grew.
They came from plants her grandmother gave her
and hers before,
borne over from some Scottish soil
through Ireland to our field.

Their fruit will bear remembrance–
feeding hungry mouths and
quenching thirst,
repaying hands that toiled
to get them here–down through their generations.

And I,
heeling them into my backyard sod
as I had seen her do before,
long to grow her graces, too,
if God will trace
the patterns of her life in me,
greening her plantings
in my weedy heart.

RBM

9. "The Lamb"

   Little lamb, who made thee?
   Dost thou know who made thee?
   Gave thee life and made thee feed
   by the stream and o'er the mead,
   Gave the clothing of delight,
   softest clothing, woolly bright,
   gave thee such a tender voice,
   making all the vales rejoice.
   Little lamb, who made thee?
   Dost thou know who made thee?

   Little lamb, I'll tell thee.
   Little lamb, I'll tell thee.
   He is called by thy name
   for He calls Himself a Lamb.
   I a child and thou a lamb,
   we are called by His Name.
   He is meek and He is mild.
   He became a little child.
   Little lamb, God bless thee.
   Little lamb, God bless thee.

   —William Blake, from *Songs of Innocence and Experience*

10. "Prose—words in their best order; poetry—the best words in their best order." —Samuel Taylor Coleridge, *Table-Talk*, July 12, 1827

11. "Poetry is the opening and closing of a door, leaving those who look through to guess about what is seen during a moment." —Carl Sandburg, *Ten Definitions of Poetry*

12. Sandburg also humorously described poetry as "a spot about half-way between where you listen and where you wonder what it was you heard."

13. Bergan Evans comments: "There have been some very unpoetical definitions [of poetry]. Isaac Barrow called poetry "a kind of ingenious nonsense," and Jeremy Bentham said that the difference between prose and poetry is that in prose all lines in a paragraph, except the last one, go clear out to the margin." —Bergan Evans, *Dictionary of Quotations*, p. 535.

14. "Poetry is the spontaneous overflow of powerful feelings; it takes its origin from emotion recollected in tranquility." —William Wordsworth, from the Preface to *The Lyrical Ballads*

15. "That summer, lying in the long grass with my head propped against the back of a saddle, with the zenith above me and the drop of distance below, I listened to the mountain silence until I could hear as far into it as the faintest clink of a cowbell. In the mountains, what might be out of sight had never really gone away. Like the mountain, that distant bell would always be there. It would keep reminding." —Eudora Welty, *One Writer's Beginnings*, P. 62

16. "It thrilled me to drink from the common dipper. The coldness, the far, unseen, unheard springs of what was in my mouth now, the iron strength of its flavor that drew my cheeks in, its fern-laced smell, all said 'mountain mountain mountain' as I swallowed. Every swallow was making me a part of being here, sealing me in place, with my bare feet planted on the mountain and sprinkled with my rapturous spills. . .," —Welty, P. 63

17. "The Charge Of The Light Brigade"
by Alfred, Lord Tennyson
(Memorializing Events in the Battle of Balaclava, October 25, 1854)

Half a league half a league,
Half a league onward,
All in the valley of Death
Rode the six hundred:
"Forward, the Light Brigade!
Charge for the guns," he said:
Into the valley of Death
Rode the six hundred.

"Forward, the Light Brigade!
Was there a man dismay'd ?
Not tho' the soldier knew
Someone had blunder'd:
Theirs not to make reply,
Theirs not to reason why,
Theirs but to do & die,
Into the valley of Death
Rode the six hundred.

Cannon to right of them,
Cannon to left of them,
Cannon in front of them
Volley'd & thunder'd;
Storm'd at with shot and shell,
Boldly they rode and well,
Into the jaws of Death,
Into the mouth of Hell
Rode the six hundred.

Flash'd all their sabres bare,
Flash'd as they turn'd in air
Sabring the gunners there,
Charging an army while
All the world wonder'd:
Plunged in the battery-smoke
Right thro' the line they broke;
Cossack & Russian
Reel'd from the sabre-stroke
Shatter'd & sunder'd.
Then they rode back, but not
Not the six hundred.

Cannon to right of them,
Cannon to left of them,
Cannon behind them
Volley'd and thunder'd;
Storm'd at with shot and shell,
While horse & hero fell,

They that had fought so well
Came thro' the jaws of Death,
Back from the mouth of Hell,
All that was left of them,
Left of six hundred.

When can their glory fade?
O the wild charge they made!
All the world wonder'd.
Honour the charge they made!
Honour the Light Brigade,
Noble six hundred!

Note: This poem, including punctuation, is reproduced from a scan of the poem written out by Tennyson in his own hand in 1864. The scan was made available online by the University of Virginia.

This poem is available in *Poems for Patriarchs*, editor, Douglas W. Phillips, The Vision Forum.

18. "Women, we must stop making apologies for God's creation order. We should give no quarter to ideas that will slay the happiness of our daughters and emasculate our sons. Let us speak the truth in love: It is wonderful to be a woman. It is glorious to be feminine. It is a privilege to do what no man can do: bring new life into this world. It is a joy and an honor to follow a godly man as his helpmeet, as together we serve the Lord." Beall Phillips, from *Verses of Virtue*, p. 93.

19. "No great thing is created suddenly." —Epictetus (c. 50-120), *Discourses*

20. A sampling of words and phrases used first by the "immortal Bard," William Shakespeare:

barefaced, civil tongue, cold comfort, eyesore, fancy free, foregone conclusion, foul play, fair play, green-eyed (as in jealous), heartsick, high time, hot-blooded, itching palm, lackluster, laughing-stock, leapfrog, lie low, long-haired, love affair, ministering angel, pitched battle, primrose path, short shrift, snow-white, stony-hearted, tongue-tied, towering passion, yeoman's service;

. . . and phrases:

> brevity is the soul of wit; there's the rub; to thine own self be true; it smells to heaven; the very witching time of night; the primrose path; though this be madness, yet there is method in it; dog will have his day; the apparel oft proclaims the man; neither a borrower nor a lender be; frailty, thy name is woman; something is rotten in the state of Denmark; the lady doth protest too much; to be or not to be; sweets for the sweet; to the manner born. . .," —Lederer, *The Miracle of Language*, p. 95, 96

21. "If you fill your speech and writing with prefabricated clichés, ramshackle abstractions and leaden expressions, you are denying the abounding creativity that is inherent in the very nature of human language. Thus it is that the manner in which you utter words, write words, and receive words [or how you listen] throughout your life determines how effectively and resourcefully you carry on the business of being a member of the human race." —Lederer, *The Miracle of Language*, p. 18 [I would add, how you may more skillfully seek to bring glory to God and inform the thinking and actions of men and nations. RBM]

22. "Keeper of the Vines"
    by Rebecca B. Morecraft

    "I am the Vine, you are the branches. . . ." —John 15:5

If she had known
as she clutched the two roots close
in her rough hands
on the ship that shivered over swells
and groaned into watery caverns
and bore her up,
scarcely breathing—

If she had known
as she stood, planted
like a small mast on the deck,
homespun sails billowing with hope
through the gray mists,
her prayers mingling with
the mocking cry of grackles rising
above Ireland's rocky coast—

If she had known, when,
transplanted and heeled-in,
she plowed her new fields
and grappled her wide dreams
down to earth,
stumbling over stones
and torn by thorns—

If she had known then
all she came to know
and what she could not know
of briary branches she would grow,
would she still have come?

23. From *On Writing Well, The Classic Guide to Writing Nonfiction*, by William Zinsser:

". . . get in the habit of using dictionaries. . . . If you have any doubt of what a word means, look it up. Learn its etymology and notice what curious branches its original root has put forth. See if it has any meanings you didn't know it had. Master the small gradations between words that seem to be synonyms. What's the difference between 'cajole' and 'wheedle,' 'blandish' and 'coax'? Get yourself a dictionary of synonyms. And don't scorn . . . *Roget's Thesaurus*. ... Look up 'villain,' for instance, and you'll be awash in such rascality as only a lexicographer could conjure back from centuries of iniquity, obliquity, depravity, knavery, profligacy, frailty, flagrancy, infamy, immorality, corruption, wickedness, wrongdoing, backsliding and sin. You'll find ruffians and riffraff, miscreants and malefactors, reprobates and rapscallions, hooligans and hoodlums, scamps and scapegraces, scoundrels and scalawags, jezebels and jades. You'll find adjectives to fit them all (foul, fiendish, devilish and diabolical), and adverbs and verbs to describe how the wrongdoers do their wrong, and cross-references leading to still other thickets of venality and vice." p. 35

"Still, there is no better friend to have around to nudge the memory than Roget's Thesaurus. It saves you the time of rummaging in your brain—that network of overloaded grooves—to find the word that's right on the tip of your tongue, where it doesn't do you any good. The Thesaurus is to the writer what a rhyming dictionary is to the songwriter—a reminder of all the choices—and you should use it with gratitude. If, having found the scalawag and the scapegrace, you want to know how they differ, then go to the dictionary." p. 35

"... bear in mind, when you are choosing words and stringing them together, how they sound. . . . such matters as rhythm [meter] and alliteration are vital to every sentence. . . E.B. White is one of my favorite stylists because I'm conscious of being with a man who cares about the cadences and sonorities of the language. I relish (in my ear) the pattern his words make as they fall into a sentence. I try to surmise how in rewriting the sentence he reassembled it to end with a phrase that will momentarily linger, or how he chose one word over another because he was after a certain emotional weight. It's the difference between, say, 'serene' and 'tranquil'—one is so soft, the other strangely disturbing because of the unusual *n* and *q*.

"Such considerations of sound and rhythm should go into everything you write. If all your sentences move at the same plodding gait, which even you recognize as deadly but don't know how to cure, read them aloud. . . . You'll begin to hear where the trouble lies. See if you can gain variety by reversing the order of a sentence, or by substituting a word that has freshness or oddity, or by altering the length of your sentences so they don't all sound as if they came out of the same machine. An occasional short sentence can carry a tremendous punch. It stays in the reader's ear. . . ." p. 36

24. Advice from Strunk and White's *Elements of Style*:

"The approach to style is by way of plainness, simplicity, orderliness, sincerity. Writing is, for most, laborious and slow. The mind travels faster than the pen; consequently, writing becomes a question of learning to make occasional wing shots, bringing down the bird of thought as it flashes by. A writer is a gunner, sometimes waiting in the blind for something to come in, sometimes roaming the countryside hoping to scare something up. Like other gunners, the writer must cultivate patience, working many covers to bring down one partridge." p. 69

"A single overstatement, wherever or however it occurs, diminishes the whole, and a single carefree superlative has the power to destroy, for readers, the object of your enthusiasm." p. 73

"Rather, very, little, pretty—these are the leeches that infest the pond of prose, sucking the blood of words. ... we should all try to do a little better, we should all be very watchful of this rule, for it is a rather important one, and we are pretty sure to violate it now and then." p. 73

"Modern writers often confuse spontaneity with genius. ... Don't be one of those writers who ... obviously has nothing to say, is showing off and directing the attention of the reader to himself, using slang with neither provocation nor ingenuity, adopting a patronizing air, is humorless, dull and empty [paraphrased]. ... [Rather, when reporting, learn to write in a way that] is compact, informative, unpretentious ... keeping a tight rein on [the] material, and by staying out of the act." p. 74

"Do not explain too much. Don't 'tell all.' Save something for your next poem or article. When writing dialogue, be sparing. Let the conversation itself disclose the speaker's manner or condition. Dialogue heavily weighted with adverbs . . . is cluttery and annoying." p. 75

"Avoid fancy words. Avoid the pretentious, the coy, and the cute. Do not be tempted by a twenty-dollar word when there is a ten-center handy, ready and able. ... The line between the fancy and the plain, between the atrocious and the felicitous, is sometimes alarmingly fine." p. 77

"Sometimes, its O.K. to break the rules of grammar. The question of [the] ear is vital. Only the writer whose ear is reliable is in a position to use bad grammar deliberately ...," pp. 77, 78

"Be clear. [The watchword for writing is Clarity!] When you become hopelessly mired in a sentence, it is best to start fresh; do not try to fight your way through against the terrible odds of syntax. Usually what is wrong is that the construction has become too involved at some point; the sentence needs to be broken apart and replaced by two or more shorter sentences. Muddiness is not merely a disturber of prose, it is also a destroyer of life, of hope: death on the highway caused by a badly worded road sign, heartbreak among lovers caused by a misplaced phrase in a well-intentioned letter, anguish of a traveler expecting to be met at a railroad station and not being met because of a slipshod telegram. Think of the tragedies that are rooted in ambiguity, and be clear! When you say something, make sure you have said it...," p. 79

"Do not inject your opinion. [Unless you are writing an 'opinion paper' with the intention to prove specific points, at least make the effort to appear neutral in your writing.]

APPENDIX A: POEMS, QUOTATIONS & OTHER INTERESTING TID-BITS

"Use figures of speech sparingly." p. 80 Too many figures of speech will make your writing as unwieldy as a heavy sword in battle, as cumbersome as a cartload of cucumbers on the battlefield, heavy like a lead balloon and as weighty as a box of dictionaries – get the picture?

"Avoid writing clichés." p. 81 Remember this phrase: Clichés are passé. I could not resist the combination of the two French words to make this point: Clichés are boring—a dime a dozen, too good to be true, not worth the paper they're written on...do you get my drift? If you've seen one, you've seen them all. They'll make you look as dumb as a doornail and cause your reader to sleep like a log. Be sly as a fox and if you start to use a cliché, drop it like a hot potato. If you don't understand what I'm saying, I guess I'll have to go the whole nine yards in my explanation. Do your word-choices or phrasing seem all too familiar? It will sound that way to your readers as well. Don't be lazy! Use your thesaurus and play with sentence structure and word choice until you say what you want in a way that will capture your reader, not put him to sleep. Write something as fresh as a daisy, cute as a button or sharp as a tack. Better safe than sorry. . . .

"Avoid writing in 'sound bites.' Unless you are writing a television commercial or magazine advertisement, don't employ ad-writers' techniques. Commercials are meant to be 'sound bites' of information that will grab the attention in a clever way with the intent of selling products. If you adopt a breezy, 'sound-bite' writing style, it may be 'catchy' to your generation but your writing will not stand the test of time as worthy literature. Sound bites belong in ads, on twitter, in texts or on Facebook. Beware of using sound bites and 'pop' language even in letters or journaling entries. Remember, your grandchildren may be reading these someday and they will have no idea what you are talking about unless you use standard, accepted terminology." p. 83

Mr. White and/or Strunk close their advice on developing a writing style with this observation:

> "Style takes its final shape more from attitudes of mind than from principles of composition. . . . style *is* the writer, and therefore what you are, rather than what you know, will at last determine your style. If you write, you must believe—in the truth and worth of the scrawl, in the ability of the reader to receive and decode the message. No one can write decently who is distrustful of the reader's intelligence, or whose attitude is patronizing." p. 84

25. Your leading sentence should "have energy, excitement, an implicit promise that something is going to happen or that some interesting information will be revealed. It should create curiosity, get the reader asking questions."
—Gary Provost, *100 Ways to Improve Your Writing: Proven Professional Techniques for Writing with Style and Power,* p. 33.

26. "Writing a short, colorful anecdote is one of the most compelling ways to begin an article, ... letter, or business proposal, and a couple of well-placed anecdotes in your longer stories will break the lock of formality and win your reader's affection as well as his or her attention." —Provost, p. 96

27. What is an anecdote? "An anecdote is a little story or incident that makes a point about your subject. . . . Anecdotes crystallize a general idea in a specific way." —Provost, p. 96

28. "There is more to seeing than observing details, which is what scientists do to gather information .... But the poet's lens is more like a prism than a telescope; more like a kaleidoscope than a microscope. For the poet takes bare fact and clothes it with meaning. The poet hears the roar on the other side of silence. ... He sees with feeling and finds words for his wonder or rage ... Poets choose words that are rich in connotation, a term that refers to emotional associations of language. [Denotation is the literal, dictionary meaning of a word.] Another way to say this is that some words are resonant, vibrating like musical sound and carrying meanings that go beyond the literal. ... To call a dandelion a weed is to condemn it. But a wildflower—now that's a thing of beauty. . . ."
—Suzanne Rhodes, *The Roar on the Other Side: A Guide for Student Poets,* p. 20.

29. "Look at life with a writer's eyes. Look for the ordinary and, through the lenses of your faith and knowledge gleaned both in His Word and His world, transform the ordinary into the extraordinary. God has done that with you and me, hasn't He? He has taken ordinary bits of clay, breathed life into us and made us vessels of honor for His use. God loves metaphor! He is the potter and we are the clay. Write about the wonder of salvation with strong imagery. Let me remind you that poetic imagery shouldn't be reserved for poems alone. We are God's poems. He is creating us into living works of art in which He can see the reflection of His face and graces. When He sees His beauty reflected in our lives, He is pleased with His handiwork." —RBM

30. "Can you see yourself as a work of art? For we are His workmanship [poem], created in Christ Jesus unto good works, which God hath before ordained that we should walk in them, Ephesians 2:10 This thought ennobles my existence and makes me live more carefully before God's face. Not only do I live, *coram Deo*, before God's watchful face, but when I remember that He is actively involved in my life transforming pain, sorrow and even sin into beauty, my life becomes a song of praise to God, enabling me to trust and praise Him even during times of tremendous pain and loss. In Isaiah 61, God tells us that He transforms ashes into beauty: To appoint unto them that mourn in Zion, to give unto them beauty for ashes, the oil of joy for mourning, the garment of praise for the spirit of heaviness; that they might be called trees of righteousness, the planting of the Lord, that He might be glorified, Isaiah 61:3." —RBM

31. "It's up to you to delight and inspire, as well as inform. God does this throughout the pages of Scripture. Just when we think we know what's coming next, we have to stop, shift gears and learn new truths. Who could have dreamed up a world made from nothing, spoken into being in six days? Who could have used for spokespersons a burning bush, a whirlwind, a donkey, sinful men and women? Who could have imagined that the Savior of the world would be born of a virgin, raised in humble surroundings as a carpenter, never to travel more than 30 miles from his home, be crucified between two thieves, buried in a borrowed tomb and then, by the power of Almighty God, be raised again in three days to reign forever at God's right hand? Who would have thought that God could love people like us, whose lifespan is as the flowers of the field that spring up in beauty today and wither and are blown away tomorrow? Who would have thought that God could love poor, broken sinners like us so much that He would give up His only Son to die for our sins? Only God could have written the story of redemption and only God can give you the eyes to see your need of a Savior and drink deeply of His rich grace. This well-spring of grace is sufficient and satisfying if you are hungry and thirsty for it. Now we have the privilege to tell others this great story of redemption as we write beautiful poems, songs and stories, articles and essays, journal entries, book reviews, letters and screenplays to His glory, magnifying His beauty for all the world to read, openly as well as 'between the lines,' in our faces, our character, our standards for writing, our careful interpretation and application of God's word to our worship and all areas of our lives." —RBM

32. "Ease, grace, freedom, simplicity and naturalness … essential qualities in every species of epistolary writing. … Make a word picture … putting into it the squirrel as well as the mountain—little things as well as great." —D. H. Jacques, quoted by Michelle Lavrin, *How to Write Love Letters*, pp. 26, 27

33. "A letter is a real affirmation. It cannot be imagined. It cannot be denied. It cannot be contradicted, unless perfidious. It's physically there, defying our insecurities and uncertainties. Unlike a telephone call, a letter can be brought out, thrillingly unfolded, time and again, to relive memories.... Years later, a letter may even deepen in meaning as layers of subsequent events and feelings are superimposed." —Lovric, p. 6

34. "We write letters because anyone can send flowers. We write letters because we want to be close to someone who is physically absent ... We write letters because they are more potent than verbal declarations. ... We write letters because they allow the reader to have their own unwitnessed reaction, to think about what is offered, and to reply in their own time. We write letters because they last...." —Lovric, p. 5

35. "Spoken words are slippery, evanescent." —Lovric, p. 5

36. "The voice flies from the lips to mingle with the winds, to be lost 'without an echo.' ... Written down, it may continue sounding on, as from a trumpet tongue, through all time...." —W.C. Fowler, quoted by Lovric, p. 7.

37. "A man is known almost as well by the words he uses as by the company he keeps. Choose both from among the best." —Daniel H. Jacques, *How to Write: A Pocket Manual of Composition and Letter-Writing: to Which are Added Forms for Letters of Introduction Notes, Cards, etc. and a Collection of Poetical Quotations* (1857), quoted by Lovrin, p. 23

38. "I have made this a rather long letter because I haven't had time to make it shorter." —Blaise Pascal, quoted by Lovric, p. 30

39. "Common sense and consideration should be the basis of etiquette and good manners." —John Quincy Adams

40. "It is an old observation that the best writers sometimes disregard the rules of rhetoric. When they do so, however, the reader will usually find in the sentence some compensating merit, attained at the cost of the violation. Unless he is certain of doing as well, he will probably do best to follow the rules. After he has learned, by their guidance, to write plain English adequate for everyday uses, let

him look for the secrets of style to the study of the masters of literature."
—William Strunk, *The Elements of Style*, from the introduction, p. 6

41. "If you want to see how active verbs give vitality to the written word, don't just go back to [more modern writers]. ... I commend the King James Bible and William Shakespeare." —William Zinsser, *Writing Well*, p. 68

42. "Writing to God's glory means, first of all, writing in such a way that bring Him honor and never shames His Name or reputation by loose or inappropriate language." —RBM

43. "When you trace the history of redemption through history, every man's story comes alive because every man's story is the story of God's hand at work in the lives of all people, events, cataclysmic occurrences, the weather, birthdays, deaths, hard times, victorious times–God is weaving your history and mine together to make a beautiful tapestry that exhibits His wisdom, knowledge, power and love." —RBM

44. "We must record God's mighty acts of providence in our lives for future generations to bring Him the glory due to His Name." —RBM

45. "Books and Soup"

    Ah, soup! The fragrance you exude will always put me in the mood
    To snuggle up before the fire and give in to my heart's desire
    To push the cares of life aside, and with my children by my side,
    Pull from the shelf a favorite tome and read aloud to them at home.
    No longer heed we winter's chill that blusters at our door to spill
    Its frosty offerings on our room and turn our brightness into gloom;
    We travel where our story leads–through jungles thick, o'er marsh and meads.
    And even if we've aches and pains—some heads that ache and ankles sprained,
    Some with complaints that beg belief—we know that soon we'll find relief
    Through stories lifting up the troops, (even the youngest with the croup),
    As we breathe deeply and re-group around the fire with books and soup.
    RBM
    February 10, 2011

46. "Everything we do is inescapably religious. We eat either for God's glory or for fleshly pleasure. Will be righteous or humanistic, serving God or man?"
—Renee DeGroot, *Health for Godly Generations*, p. 47.

47. "Everything we do for the glory of God is a 'hallelujah-ing' to Jehovah."
—Joe Morecraft, III

48. "Grammar isn't the only key to good sentence writing, of course. Word choice, common sense, passion, information—all these elements and more are essential. Yet all great writing has one thing in common. It starts with a sentence. The sentence is a microcosm of any written work, and understanding it means understanding writing itself—how to structure ideas, how to emphasize what's important, how to make practical use of grammar, how to cut the [unnecessary], and, above all, how to serve the almighty Reader."
—June Casagrande, *It Was the Best of Sentences, It Was the Worst of Sentences*, p. 6

49. "We must train ourselves to feel pleasure, liking, disgust, and hatred at those things which really are pleasant, likeable, disgusting, and hateful. We must constantly ask ourselves whether the things we put before our eyes train us in this way, or just further distort our ability to appreciate [what is] good, true, and beautiful," from the Harris brothers The Rebelution e-mail of February 3, 2011

50. Admonitions from Scripture on speaking with grace:

> "The heart of the righteous ponders how to answer; but the mouth of the wicked pours out evil things." —Proverbs 15:28, NASV

> "A gentle answer turns away wrath, but a harsh word stirs up anger."
> —Proverbs 15:1, NASV

> "A soothing tongue is a tree of life, but perversion in it crushes the spirit."
> —Proverbs 1:4, NASV

> "In the mouth of the foolish is a rod for his back, but the lips of the wise will preserve them." —Proverbs 13:3, NASV

> "He who restrains his words has knowledge, and he who has a cool spirit is a man of understanding." —Proverbs 17:27, NASV

51. Here are some wise sayings about words:

    "Sharp words make more wounds than surgeons can heal."

    "Words are the most powerful drug used by mankind." —Rudyard Kipling

    "All words are pegs to hang ideas on." —Henry Ward Beecher

    "A word is dead when it is said, some say. I say it just begins to live that day."
    —Emily Dickinson

    "As a man grows older and wiser, he talks less and says more."

52. "We give thanks , [dear Lord], for language—the human essence, the skin of thought, more to the mind than light is to the eye. May we try not only to talk, but to say something; not only to hear, but to listen; not only to write, but to communicate. May our thoughts and aspirations become words that serve to build bridges from mind to mind and from heart to heart, creating a fellowship of those who would hold fast to that which is good."
    —Richard Lederer, *The Miracle of Language*, p. 243

53. "A great many husbands are spoiled by mismanagement. ... [Some women keep their husbands in hot water.] Others let them freeze, by their carelessness and indifference. Some keep them in a stew, by irritating ways and words; others roast them; some keep them in a pickle all their lives. Now it is not to be supposed that any husband will be good managed in this way—turnips wouldn't. [Neither would] onions or cabbage; husbands won't [either]; but they are really delicious when properly treated."
    —Elizabeth Strong Worthington, *How to Cook a Husband*, 1898

54. "The Power of Short Words"
    (a poem consisting of only one-syllable words)
    by Joseph Addison Alexander (1809-1860)

    Think not that strength lies in the big round word,
    Or that the brief and plain must needs be weak.
    To whom can this be true who once has heard
    The cry for help, the tongue that all men speak
    When want or woe or fear is in the throat,
    So that each word gasped out is like a shriek
    Pressed from the sore heart, or a strange, wild note

Sung by some fay or fiend? There is a strength
Which dies if stretched too far or spun too fine,
Which has more height than breadth, more depth
Than length.
Let but this force of thought and speech be mine,
And he that will may take the sleek fat phrase,
Which glows and burns not, though it gleam and shine;
Light, but not heat—a flash, but not a blaze!

Nor mere strength is it that the short word boasts:
It serves of more than fight or storm to tell—
The roars of waves that clash on rock bound coasts,
The crash of tall trees when the wild winds swell,
The roar of guns, the groans of men that die
On blood stained fields. It has a voice as well
For them that far off on their sick-beds lie,
For them that weep, for them that mourn the dead;
For them that laugh, and dance, and clap the hand.
To Joy's quick step as well as Grief's slow tread,
The sweet, plain words we learn at first keep time;
And though the theme be sad or gay or grand,
With each, with all, these may be made to chime,
In thought or speech or song, in prose or rhyme.

55. Shakespeare on Good Elocution: (This selection is Hamlet's address to the players in the tragedy of *Hamlet*, Act III. Scene 2). "Speak the speech, I pray you, as I pronounced it to you, trippingly on the tongue; but if you mouth it, as many of our players do, I had as life the town-crier spoke my lines...."

56. "A song for simplicity"
    by Luci Shaw

There are some things that should be as they are:
plain, unadorned, common and all-complete;
things not in a clutter, not in a clump,
unmuddled and unmeddled with;
the straight, the smooth, the salt, the sour, the sweet.
For all that's timeless, untutored, untailored and untooled;
for innocence unschooled;

for unploughed prairies, primal snow and sod,
water unmuddied, wind unruled,
for these, thank God.

Singly and strongly, from each separate star
a brightness pricks the retina from far
to near. And for clear eyes to see
deep space and dark infinity
with an untroubled gaze,
give praise.

With both hands unjewelled and with unbound hair
beauty herself stands unselfconscious where
she is enough to have, and worth the always holding.
The mind perceiving her, the heart enfolding
echoes the unchanged pattern from above
that praises God for loveliness, and love.

Glory again to God for word and phrase
whose magic, matching the mind's computed leap,
lands on the lip of truth,
(plain as a stone well's mouth, and as deep)
and for the drum, the bell, the flute, the harp, the bird,
for music, Praise! that speaks without a word.

As for the rightness to be found
in the unembellished square and the plain round,
in geometric statement of a curve
respond! without reserve
but with astonishment that there's for every man
one point in time, one plainly drafted plan,
and in your unique place
give glory for God's grace.

All this from him whose three-in-one
so simply brought to birth
from the red earth
a son.

All our complexity, diversity, décor
facet the gem, encrust the clarity.
So pierce you now the opalescent glaze
till all your praise
rises to him in whom you find no flaw.

Luci Shaw, from *Polishing the Petoskey Stone*, p. 79.

57. "The rule is: the word 'it's' (with apostrophe) stand for 'it is' or 'it has.' If the word does not stand for 'it is' or 'it has' then what you require is 'its' (without apostrophe). This is extremely easy to grasp. Getting yours ites mixed up is the greatest solecism in the world of punctuation. No matter that you have a PhD. ... If you still persist in writing, 'Good food at it's best,' you deserve to be struck by lightning, hacked up on the spot and buried in an unmarked grave."
—Lynn Truss, *Eats, Shoots and Leaves*, pp. 43, 44.

58. In the preface of her excellent book, *Woe is I*, Patricia O'Conner, a former editor at The New York Times Book Review, says: "... good English is good English, whether in an e-mail or a letter or an essay or a book." (from the preface, p. xii.)

59. "Graceful, strong writing to the glory of God will bring a smile to His face and beautify your life as well as He sees fit to bless it to make a difference in the world in your lifetime and perhaps for generations to follow." —RBM

60. "We need to learn to write as mature, well-spoken adults who know how to express our thoughts in our own unique voices and still retain a freshness of expression and the wonder of a child." —RBM

61. "English is a glorious invention, one that gives us endless possibilities for expressing ourselves. Grammar is there to help, to clear up ambiguities and prevent misunderstandings. Any 'rule' of grammar that gets in the way or doesn't make sense or creates problems instead of solving them probably isn't a rule at all." —Patricia O'Conner, *Woe is I*, p. xiii.

62. "To me as a child, Sunday dinners were about the beauty of the ordinary and the sanctity of Sunday and family. ... Sunday dinner was set apart. ... After the morning church service each Sunday, my parents, brother, and I journeyed the twenty miles

through the cornfields to my grandparents' house. We gathered with uncles and aunts and cousins around the large rectangular table in the kitchen. ... We would eat and talk during dinner, discussing Sunday sermons and news from town. ... Our custom at every meal was to pray before we ate and then afterward read the Bible or a devotional book and pray again. This is what I remember the most about Sunday dinner: my grandfather reading the Bible. . . . he read slowly and carefully, almost haltingly, and with a sense of reverence and awe. And through his reading I heard the Scriptures afresh—especially when he read the Psalms. To me, it was as if God spoke."
—Gina Vos, quoted in *A Return to Sunday Dinner* by Russell Cronkhite

63. Hungarian Goulash Soup
(from *Soup*, editor Michael Fullalove, Covent Garden Books, American edition by DK Publishing, New York, New York, 2011, p. 308.)

Serves: 6-8
Prep time: 15 mins.
Cook time: 2 hours
Freezes: up to 3 months
Utensils: Chopping block, Chopping knife, Heavy stew pot, Heavy skillet, and Measuring cups & spoons

Ingredients

4 Tbsp. olive oil
4 large potatoes
2 cloves garlic
Salt and freshly ground pepper
1 tsp. caraway seeds (I add 1 tsp. cumin)
4 Tbsp. tomato purée
Sour cream and parsley or chives to garnish

1 ½ lbs. onions
3 medium carrots
1 ½ lbs. chuck steak, cubed
2 Tbsp. paprika
1 tsp cayenne pepper (optional)
1 qt. beef stock

Method
- Coarsely chop two large sweet onions.
- Heat three tablespoons of the olive oil in a large heavy stock pot or stew pot over medium heat.
- Add the chopped onions and cook, stirring so as not to burn.
- When the onions are browned, add chopped potatoes and carrots, cut into chunks. Stir into the onions and allow to cook for two-three minutes to retain their color.

- Then add the garlic, stir for about two minutes and remove from the heat.
- Put one tablespoon olive oil in a heavy skillet and heat on medium heat.
- Add the cubed steak and brown it on all sides.
- Season with salt and add to the onion, garlic mixture in the stockpot.
- Add the rest of the spices and tomato puree.
- Return the pot to the heat and cook for five minutes, stirring constantly.
- Pour in the beef stock. Cover with a lid and simmer gently for 1 ¾ hours.
- Season to taste with salt and freshly ground black pepper.
- Serve in bowls and garnish with a dollop of sour cream sprinkled with a dash of either paprika or cayenne pepper for color. (A sprig of parsley or a few chopped chives may also be added for a garnish of color.)

64. "A Mighty Fortress is our God"

A mighty fortress is our God; A bulwark, never failing.
Our helper, He amid the flood of mortal ills prevailing.
For still our ancient foe doth seek to work us woe;
His craft and power are great and armed with cruel hate,
On earth is not his equal.

Did we in our own strength confide, our striving would be losing.
Were not the right man on our side, the man of God's own choosing.
Dost ask who that may be? Christ Jesus, it is He.
Lord Sabaoth His name, from age to age the same;
And He must win the battle.

And though this world with devils filled should threaten to undo us,
We will not fear, for God hath willed His truth to triumph through us.
The prince of darkness grim, we tremble not for him;
His rage we can endure, for lo, his doom is sure.
One little word shall fell him.

That Word above all earthly powers, no thanks to them, abideth.
The Spirit and the gifts are ours through Him Who with us sideth.
Let goods and kindred go, this mortal life also.

The body they may kill; God's truth abideth still.
His kingdom is forever.

—Martin Luther's Reformation Hymn

65. Below is a portion of an essay presented by Rev. Edward Everett Hale, born in 1822, on the subject of concise writing and speaking. Our commentator in Swinton's *Fifth Reader and Speaker*, says this about him: "[He was] an American essayist [whose] style is clear, pointed and vivacious." See if you agree:

"Whenever I am going to write anything, I find it best to think first what I am going to say. This is a lesson which nine writers out of ten have never learned. . . . you may divide literature into two great classes of books. The smaller class of the two consists of the books written by people who had something to say. They had in life learned something, or seen something, or done something which they really wanted and needed to tell to other people. They told it. And their writings make, perhaps, a twentieth part of the printed literature of the world. It is the part which contains all that is worth reading. The other nineteen-twentieths make up the other class.

"In learning to write, our first rule is: Know what you want to say. The second rule is: Say it. That is, do not begin by saying something else which you think will lead up to what you want to say. ... Thirdly, and always, use your own language. I mean the language you are accustomed to use in daily life. If your every-day language is not fit for a letter or for print, it is not fit for talk. And if, by any series of joking and fun, at school or at home, you have got into the habit of using slang in talk, which is not fit for print, why, the sooner you get out of it the better."

[Fourth] A short word is better than a long one. Here is a piece of weak English. It is not bad in other regards, but simply weak:

> 'Entertaining unlimited confidence in your intelligent and patriotic devotion to the public interest, and being conscious of no motives on my part which are separable from the honor and advancement of my country, I hope it may be my privilege to deserve and secure, not only your cordial co-operation in great public measure, but also those relations of mutual confidence and regard, which it is always so desirable to cultivate between

members of co-ordinate branches of the government.'

Taken as an exercise for translation into shorter words—striking out the unnecessary words, Rev. Hale adapted the 81-word declamation into a 35-word statement:

> 'I have full trust in you. I am sure that I seek only the honor and advance of the country. I hope, therefore, I may earn your respect and regard, while we heartily work together.'" —Swinton's *Fifth Reader and Speaker*, pp. 33-37

66. Why improve your vocabulary?

    a. If you have a wide vocabulary, your reading comprehension will be ahead of the game–you will grasp concepts and instantly 'translate' the meaning of the words into your comfort zone.

    b. You will be better able to express yourself in more cogent terms. In other words, you will learn to be precise and accurate.

    c. Your brain will begin to make vocabulary connections that allow you to write with deeper and broader imagery.

67. "Jesus Savior, Pilot Me"

Jesus Savior, pilot me, over life's tempestuous sea.
Unknown waves around me roll, hiding rock and treacherous shoal.
Chart and compass come from Thee. Jesus Savior, pilot me.

As a mother stills her child, Thou canst hush the ocean wild.
Boisterous waves obey Thy will when Thou sayst to them, "Be still!"
Wondrous Sovereign of the sea, Jesus Savior, pilot me.

When at last I near the shore, and the fearful breakers roar
'Twixt me and the peaceful rest, then while learning on Thy breast,
May I hear Thee say to me, "Fear not, I will comfort Thee.
Fear not, child, I'll comfort thee."

Edward Hopper, 1871

68. "In the preface of her excellent book, *Woe is I*, Patricia O'Conner, a former editor at The New York Times Book Review, says: "...good English is good English, whether in an e-mail or a letter or an essay or a book." (from the preface, p. xii.)

"I couldn't agree more! As I've said many times in several different ways throughout these webinar sessions, we must remember when we write that we live *coram Deo*, before the face of God. He is, as it were, 'reading over our shoulders,' taking note of our thoughts put into words. Whatever we do should be an offering to Jehovah, committed to Him for His glory. Will He be pleased with our offerings? I'm conscious of many people when I write: Will my husband approve of any theological comments I've made? (He's my favorite theologian next to the Apostle Paul.) Would my grandfather like it? (He was the major influence in my life for great literature.) Would my mother approve? (She still writes for a local newspaper at age 82.)If it's poetry, would my sister Judy Rogers, songwriter par excellence, approve the meter? But the overriding and undergirding thought in my mind is: Does this bring glory to God?" RBM

69. "A word here about legitimate circular reasoning. Have you ever thought about why we believe the Bible is God's holy, inspired and perfect word? Because He says it is. Where does He say that? Right, in the Bible. Why do we believe the Bible? Because in it, God reveals Himself as its Author and says it's trustworthy—it is the self-authenticating Word of God. Here's an example of perfectly safe circular reasoning." —RBM

70. Portions of Psalm 16 from the 1912 Psalter:

To thee, O Lord, I fly and on Thy help depend;
Thou art my Lord and King most high;
do Thou my soul defend. A heritage for me Jehovah will remain;
my portion rich and full is He, my right He will maintain.
The lot to me that fell is beautiful and fair;
the heritage in which I dwell is good beyond compare.
I praise the Lord above Whose counsel guides aright;
my heart instructs me in His love in seasons of the night.
I keep before me still the Lord Whom I have proved;
at my right hand He guards from ill, and I shall not be moved.
Life's pathway Thou wilt show, to Thy right hand wilt guide,
Where streams of pleasure ever flow and boundless joys abide

71. "Jesus, Priceless Treasure"
    Original Trinity Hymnal, #550
    (based on I Peter 2:3)

    Jesus, priceless treasure,
    Fount of purest pleasure,
    Truest friend to me:
    Ah, how long in anguish
    Shall my spirit languish,
    Yearning, Lord, for thee?
    Thine I am, O spotless Lamb!
    I will suffer naught to hide thee,
    Naught I ask beside thee.

    In thine arms I rest me;
    Foes who would molest me
    Cannot reach me here.
    Though the earth be shaking,
    Ev'ry heart be quaking,
    Jesus calms my fear.
    Lightnings flash and thunders crash;
    Yet, though sin and hell assail me,
    Jesus will not fail me.

    Satan, I defy thee;
    Death, I now decry thee;
    Fear, I bid thee cease.
    World, thou shalt not harm me
    Nor thy threats alarm me
    While I sing of peace.
    God's great pow'r guards ev'ry hour;
    Earth and all its depths adore him,
    Silent bow before him.

    Hence with earthly treasure!
    Thou art all my pleasure,
    Jesus, all my choice.
    Hence, thou empty glory!

Naught to me thy story,
Told with tempting voice.
Pain or loss or shame or cross
Shall not from my Saviour move me,
Since he deigns to love me.

Hence, all fear and sadness!
For the Lord of gladness,
Jesus, enters in.
Those who love the Father,
Though the storms may gather,
Still have peace within.
Yea, whate'er I here must bear,
Thou art still my purest pleasure,
Jesus, priceless treasure.

Words by: Johann Franck, 1655
Translated by: Catherine Winkworth, 1863
Music by: Johann Cruger, 1649
Harmonized by: J. S. Bach, 1685-1750

72. "Whate'er My God Ordains is Right"
    Original Trinity Hymnal, p. 94

Whate'er my God ordains is right: holy His will abideth.
I will be still whatev'er He doth, and follow where He guideth.
He is my God; though dark my road, He holds me that I shall not fall:
Wherefore to Him I leave it all.

Whate'er my God ordains is right: He never will deceive me;
He leads me by the proper path; I know He will not leave me.
I take, content, what He hath sent; His hand can turn my griefs away,
And patiently I wait his day.

Whate'er my God ordains is right: Though now this cup, in drinking,
May bitter seem to my faint heart, I take it all unshrinking.
My God is true; each morn anew sweet comfort yet shall fill my heart,
And pain and sorrow shall depart.

Whate'er my God ordains is right: Here shall my stand be taken.
Though sorrow, need, or death be mine, yet am I not forsaken.
My Father's care is round me there; He holds me that I shall not fall:
And so to Him I leave it all.

Words: Samuel Rodigast, 1675
Translated by Catherine Winkworth, 1829-1878

APPENDIX B
Sources & Resources

Note: As a Christian reader, writer, mother, grandmother and teacher, I have attempted to use as much discernment as possible before listing a book. If I think a book offers enough worthy information, it appears on the list, which is not intended to be comprehensive, by the way. However, always read anything on this list or any other recommended list with your Christian mindset intact, ready to sift and sort. Glean what is good, wholesome, pure, lovely and true and let the wind blow the chaff away. —RBM

Books on Writing Well and Quotation Sources
[Many of these books were used as my resources during the webinar sessions.]

The Roar on the Other Side: A Guide for Student Poets, by Suzanne Rhodes, Canon Press, Moscow, ID, 2000.

100 Ways to Improve Your Writing, by Gary Provost, Penguin Books, New York, NY, 1985.

Writing to God's Glory: A Comprehensive Creative Writing Course, From Crayon to Quill, by Jill Bond, published by Homeschool Press, Elkton, MD, 1997.

Any Child Can Write, by Harvey S. Wiener, Oxford University Press, New York, NY, 2003.

One Writer's Beginnings, by Eudora Welty, Warner Books, Inc., New York, NY, 1983.

Word Power Made Easy, by Norman Lewis, Pocket Books, New York, NY, 1949.

Painless Grammar, by Rebecca Elliott, Barron's, Hauppauge, NY, 2006.

On Writing Well, by William Zinsser, Harper Collins Publishers, New York, NY, 2006.

The Grammar Devotional, by Mignon Fogarty, Henry Holt and Co., New York, NY, 2009.

It Was the Best of Sentences, It Was the Worst of Sentences: A Writer's Guide to Crafting Killer Sentences, by June Casagrande, Random House, Inc., New York, NY, 2010.

Eats, Shoots & Leaves, by Lynne Truss, Gotham Books, New York, NY, 2003.

100 Words Every High School Graduate Should Know, from the editors of the American Heritage Dictionaries, Houghton Mifflin Co., Boston, MA, 2003.

The Only Grammar Book You'll Ever Need, by Susan Thurman, Adams Media, Avon, MA, 2002.

Literature Through the Eyes of Faith, by Susan V. Gallagher & Roger Lundin, HarperCollins Publishers, New York, NY, 1989.

Learning Grammar Through Writing, by Sandra M. Bell and James I. Wheeler, Educators Publishing Service, Inc., Cambridge, MA, 1993.

The New International Webster's Pocket Grammar Dictionary of the English Language, Trident Press International, USA, 2002.

Smart's Handbook of Effective Writing, by Walter K. Smart and Daniel R. Lang, Harper & Brothers, USA, 1943.

Woe is 'I': The Grammarphobe's Guide to Better English in Plain English, by Patricia T. O'Conner, Riverhead Books, New York, NY, 2009.

The Elements of Style, original 1920 edition, by William Strunk, Jr., Dover Publications, Mineola, NY, 2006.

The Writer's Handbook, 110 Chapters on How to Write, Edited by Sylvia K. Burack, The Writer, Inc., Boston, MA, 1998. Much of the outline and some of the definitions in this webinar are taken from *Smart's Handbook of Effective Writing*, by Walter K. Smart and Daniel R. Lang, published by Harper and Brothers, New York and London, third edition, 1943.

Wise Words and Quotes, by Vern McLellan, Tyndale House Publishers, Wheaton, Ill, 1998.

Elocution

Swinton's Fifth Reader and Speaker, Ivison, Blakeman, Taylor & Co., publishers, New York, NY, 1883.

Speaking the Truth in Love: A Modern Primer on Private and Public Discourse, by Rebecca B. Morecraft, manuscript currently unpublished but underway.

Useful Books About Words

An American Dictionary of the English Language, 1828 edition, by Noah Webster, The Vision Forum, Inc., San Antonio, TX.

Roget's Thesaurus (This is available in many different editions and formats.)

An Almanac of Words at Play, by Willard R. Espy, Clarkson N. Potter, Inc., Publisher, New York, NY, 1975.

The Complete Word Book: The Practical Guide to Anything and Everything You Need to Know About Words and How to Use Them, by Mary A. DeVrie, Barnes & Noble Books, New York, NY, 1991.

The Miracle of Language, by Richard Lederer, Pocket Books, New York, NY, 1991.

Books that Recommend Books

The Book Tree: A Christian Reference for Children's Literature, by Elizabeth McCallum and Jane Scott, Canon Press, Moscow ID, 2001.

Honey for a Child's Heart, by Gladys Hunt, Zondervan, Grand Rapids, MI, 2002.

Recommended Poetry Books

Roots & Vines, A Collection of Poems, by Rebecca B. Morecraft, self-published, Atlanta, GA, 1999.

Verses of Virtue, compiled and edited by Elizabeth Beall Phillips, The Vision Forum, Inc., San Antonio, Texas, 2002.

Poems for Patriarchs, compiled and edited by Douglas W. Phillips, The Vision Forum, Inc., San Antonio, Texas, 2000.

Listen to the Green, by Luci Shaw, Harold Shaw Publishers, Wheaton, Illinois, 1971.

The Best Loved Poems of the American People, selected by Hazel Felleman, Doubleday, New York, NY, 1936.

Kipling, A Selection of His Stories and Poems, John Beecroft, Doubleday & Company, Garden City, NY, 1932.

Books on Letter-Writing and Related Topics

Gift of a Letter, by Alexandra Stoddard, Doubleday Publishers, New York, NY, 1990.

How to Write Love Letters, by Michelle Lovric, Shooting Star Press, Inc., New York, NY, 1995. (**Disclaimer:** While there is much good to be gleaned from the pages of this little book, there are illustrations and other materials which some may not consider suitable. Use discernment and sift through the grid of Christian morality—always.)

The Art of Thank You: Crafting Notes of Gratitude, by Connie Leas, MJF Books, New York, NY, 2002.

Crane's Blue Book of Stationery: The Styles and Etiquette of Letters, Notes and Invitations, edited by Steven L. Feinberg, Doubleday, New York, NY, 1989.

Suggested Reading for Collections of Letters and Journals

Diary of a Southern Refugee During the War, by Judith B. McGuire, Sprinkle Publications, Harrisonburg, VA.

The Children of Pride: Selected Letters of the Family of the Rev. Dr. Charles Colcock Jones from the Years 1860-1868; A New, Abridged Edition [Abridged], by Robert Manson Myers, Vail-Ballou Press, Binghamton, NY, 1978.

Best of Covered Wagon Women, Vol.s 1 & 2, edited by Kenneth L. Holmes, University of Oklahoma Press: Norman, OK, 2008.

Familiar Letters of John Adams and His Wife Abigail Adams, During the Revolution, by Charles Francis Adams, Hurd and Houghton, Cambridge: The Riverside Press, 1876.

Of Plymouth Plantation, by William Bradford.

The Journals of Captain Cook, by James Cook

The Journals of Lewis and Clark, by William Clark

The Diary of Kenneth MacCrae, by Kenneth MacCrae (a Scottish preacher at the turn of the 20th century)

The Diary of John Evelyn, by John Evelyn (a Puritan businessman)

The Letterbook of Eliza Lucas Pinckney (selected portions available from Vision Forum as an audio book)

APPENDIX C
Pre-Writing & Story Ideas

Here is a sample from Jill Bond's book *Writing to God's Glory: A Comprehensive Creative Writing Course from Crayon to Quill*. I hope you will profit from her ideas on these pages and purchase the book in order to expand your capabilities.

Pre-Writing
(The Process of Writing)

How many hours do you invest in a writing challenge before you ever allow your fingers to touch a keyboard?

If you begin to write first, your words and thoughts will be random, unstructured, and very difficult to follow. Your illustrations will be contrived. Your prose will be formulated, your conclusions unproven, your characters flat, and worst of all, your theology shaky.

Think first. Better yet pray first.

For starters, develop a two-for-one ratio in your pre-writing skills: for every hour you will spend putting words onto paper, spend two hours pre-writing. As your talent is blessed, you'll want to raise the ratio.

Pre-Writing Stage One: Idea Generation

You have an idea. Great! Allow it room to grow.

Nurture it with prayer. Where does the Lord want it to go? What does the Lord want it to become? How can He use it for His purpose?

Pray for words. Pray for concepts. Pray for linking ideas. Pray for characters. Pray for prose. Pray.

Pre-Writing Stage Two: Research

Study. Study His Word.

Research His Word to match your concept with his Truth. Don't be flippant about your theme. Don't be cavalier about the plot. Don't promote satan's agenda.

Pre-Writing Stage Three: Right Brain Work

Talk it through. Bounce it off your family and friends. Make yourself accountable.

Jotting down ideas, notes, research, or phrasing is all part of pre-writing. Don't lose those gems.

Don't bury that inspiration.

Pre-Writing Stage Four: Pre-Production

Formulate your story. Formulate it so it won't appear to be formula writing.

See separate sections on casting (page 143), setting (page 145), and timing (page 147).

Pre-Writing Stage Five: Blocking

No flats are painted yet. The music might not be completely scored. the costumes are still being fitted. Yet, the director assembles the cast for a "blocking party." he has the characters walk through the script.

In the same way, you, as the director of your story, need to block you characters through your story-line. Some might refer to this as outlining.

You might jot down bits and pieces of ideas. Fine. Just prepare in your mind, with notes for reference, the framework for the plot.

At this stage, don't worry about detail. As you begin to write, details will fit together and develop as you go.

As you write, you'll be glad you invested the mental energy in pre-writing. Your story will have depth. It will have emotion. It will be professional. It won't have the style of an amateur who hates writing. It will sing with the glory of God.

"Cast thy burden up the LORD, and He shall sustain thee: He shall never suffer the righteous to be moved." —Psalm 55:22

Casting
(Character Development)

Develop three-dimensional characters. Imagine their life stories. Know more about them than you'll ever tell the reader. Go beyond the standard demographics of age, race, height, weight, and head-of-household statistics. Develop them into human beings:

- What do they look like?
- Where did they go to school?
- What early childhood memories affected their attitudes about adulthood?
- What are their favorite movies?
- What have they names their pets?
- Why don't they have any pets?
- What do they read?
- What are their salvation testimonies?
- When they are alone, what do they do?
- What are their besetting sins?
- What were their dreams when they were ten years old?
- Why haven't they reached them?
- What are their styles in clothing, cars, dwellings?
- What will they NOT eat under any circumstances?
- What would they kill for?
- What will get them off the couch and out the door?
- Who influences their decisions?

- How emotional are they?
- What kinds of words do they use in their business, with friends, with their parents?

That's right, develop more than you'll ever tell the reader. But if you can see your characters, if you can hear them, if you can crawl into their skins, then so will your reader. You'll have plausible characters. You'll have characters that can reach others. You'll have the start of a good story or article.

Now, how are you going to show the reader these traits? How are you going to introduce the reader to your imaginary friends? How much are you going to reveal? How much will you leave for the reader's own vision? How are you going to invite the reader to get personally involved in the story?

Here are some ways to introduce your characters to your readers:

- Dialogue
- Foils
- Action
- Plot
- Events
- Setting
- Timing

A fun game to play is to actually cast the parts. Pretend you are the casting director and this story is going to be made into a mini-series. Millions of people will watch it. You want just the right person to play each part. Now, with your knowledge of actors, actresses, characters from history, and people you know—cast the parts.

- Would your dad play the lead?
- Would Harrison Ford play the hero?
- Would your little sister make a good Melanie?
- How about your piano teacher? Would she make a Mrs. Sweetvoice?
- Do you want someone like Walter Cronkite or Robin Williams to play the part of the Sunday School Teacher?
- Would you cast your grandmother, or Helen Hayes, as the pastor's wife?
- Who would you hire to play your part in the story?
- Should the dog be Lassie, Benji, or Beethoven?
- Should you hire the Sheriff of Nottingham or Omar Sharif as the rogue?

- Errol, Arnold, or Ernest?
- Shari, Cher, or Chevy?

Worksheets 3 and 4 (pages 289-291) gives you room to develop your characters. Make a separate sheet for each character. Cut pictures out of magazines that go with the character. Draw things that the character would carry, have, or want. Write down words that the character would use: "The Hero's Vocabulary."

Make your characters real.

"Thine eyes did see my substance, yet being unperfect; and in thy book all my members were written, which in continuance were fashioned, when as yet there was none of them." —Psalm 139:16

APPENDIX D
Recommended Reading Lists & More

"I cannot live without my books." —Thomas Jefferson to John Adams, 1815

When you sow the seeds of gleaned words in your writer's garden, you will reap bountiful results as you write. One of the best ways to accomplish this goal is to read great literature. I use the term "great" not in terms of every reader's opinion, because each of us has standards of "greatness" according to individual preferences. I mean books, stories and poems that have passed the test of time and remain on lists developed by respected academia.

Literary snobs, you say? Well, only in the sense that most of them, whether you agree with their choices or not, have invested time and mental energy into the task of reading the good, the bad and the mediocre and have learned, by comparison, how to sort the categories. When I was in college 45 years ago, a young lady raised her hand and asked my old English professor why we had to read such boring old books. His reply has stayed with me. "Miss I____," his icy tones surely frosted the girl as he peered disdainfully over his wire-rimmed glasses at her. "Great literature has already proved itself worthy. It is now you who must prove yourself against it."

Most "Great Books" list-makers are teachers in colleges and high schools or homeschool groups who have suffered through many a dull research paper, story or poem and despaired of ever reading anything reasonably creative or even grammatically correct. And then, unexpectedly, that well-written, innovative paper or story is handed them and their very existence seems vindicated! Somebody got it!! Maybe it took patiently red-marking the rough drafts three times to get them there, but cooperatively, something wonderful clicked in the mind and moved onto the paper. This is every English teacher's moment of glory.

Sadly, some of the best examples of well-written English literature are works that I cannot recommend on the whole and have chosen not to read myself, although I will occasionally excerpt something from this writing for the sake of example. Many brilliant writers write from an anti-Christian worldview. We could spend hours arguing and discussing the advantages or dangers in exposing ourselves to articulate, persuasive literature that belittles God and the Bible. Especially dangerous are those well-written works based on anti-Christian principles which may draw in the unsuspecting reader under the guise of innocence.

When I compiled this list of recommended books, I sought the assistance of valued friends who have hundreds of years of solid Christian teaching in their cumulative experience. Many of the recommendations listed here come from them along with my own preferences. However, I decided to look through other recommended book sources, including several from the secular scene. Invariably, I encountered stories that encourage an "open mind" regarding practices and beliefs that deliberately and self-consciously seek to destroy Biblical standards for moral choices and beliefs. Children's books from the very earliest stages either promote or degrade Christian morality and beliefs. There is no "neutral position" in this God-breathed universe! Let the reader beware.

With these principles in mind, although my recommendations are thoughtfully selected, I make disclaimers occasionally if I think there may be some objectionable areas in a book that could be skipped or explained, like putting an otherwise good movie on "fast-forward" in places. Some books are worth reading despite their flaws. However, for the most part, that won't be necessary because there are enough great books to keep us busy with Christian themes or with Christian principles as their basis. We won't need to wander far-afield.

Not all good books are old and not all old books are good. Why should we be interested in learning how to write if we can only recommend old books? My grandson, Charlie, has an amazing speaking vocabulary at age two. He loves books and words. He knows what he doesn't like as well. He will look at our beloved rare books, placed high on shelves and comment: "Hmm, old, boring books. Don't want to see those." I suspect, with the parents, aunts, uncles, grandparents and even great and great-great grandparents Charlie inherited, it won't be long until his interest in "boring old books" will be kindled.

You, dear writing friend, will write from the wealth of words and ideas you have stored in your head and heart. That is a given. Therefore, I recommend that you read good books, old and new, so that your word-well is filled with a fountain of words that spring up as you need them, enabling you to create vivid, satisfying word pictures or to find exactly the right word that communicates precisely what you mean to say. As you read great literature, almost unconsciously you will enrich this store of words and formulate ideas that will inform your writing style. As you absorb the vocabularies and styles of writers you admire, your voice will be freed rather than confined by them. Since your writing is shaped by your presuppositions, word choices and the expression of your unique ideas, your voice, not those of the writers you have read, will eventually be the voice your reader hears. This is called the creative process. It's almost a miracle!

More Thoughts on Book Recommendations

I used to trust people who said to me: "Oh, that movie/book is fine—there's nothing objectionable in it at all." To my dismay, this was often not the case. I have come to realize that, even for Christians, the bars are set in different places for what is allowable and what is objectionable. This moves me to apologize if I have listed a book which you would decide not to read, either because of content or perspective. Please allow your own discernment to hold sway. As my Granny would say, "Use your sanctified gumption!"

We are each responsible before God to make intelligent, discerning decisions in all areas of life. I am still a work in progress. Even the Christian authors I read and recommend are still "sinners, saved by grace," struggling against our individual ingrained sinful attitudes and perspectives. Even with my best efforts, I will sometimes err on one side or the other. I realize that I am more than likely omitting something flawed that is otherwise praise-worthy or including something that falls beneath the Biblical standard set by God: "Whatever is true, honorable, right, pure, lovely and of good repute. If there is any excellence and if anything worthy of praise, dwell on these things" (Philippians 4:8, ASV, paraphrased). Please forgive me for this all too human error in judgment.

Some of you may wonder why I haven't included books by C. S. Lewis and J.R.R. Tolkien. Their writings had a profound influence for good on me as a young reader. I took a mini-semester course called "The Inklings" in college in which we examined the writings of C. S. Lewis, J. R. R. Tolkien and Charles Williams, the prominent members of this literary society. I am very aware that many of my readers have problems with reading about wizards, witches and magic which dominate much of the writings of these incredibly gifted authors. Does that mean that I won't read some of their writings? No, I have read and enjoyed many of their books (not all are my favorites but were enjoyable when I read them). I believe I understand their basic philosophies (which are not identical in the least), having studied their lives and what influenced them and why they wrote as they did. I don't share many of the ideas which they embraced nor would I include the occult or pagan mythological creatures in my writing; but I don't believe I am sinning when I read their writings with a critical attitude. I know that as I sift what they wrote through the grid of Biblical analysis, I honor the Lord. However, I would not recommend these or any books of this genre to immature readers who have yet to develop the "grid" necessary to discern good from evil.

Although the Biblical standards are clear, in my opinion, the decisions we make concerning what we will or will not read fall in the area of "Christian liberty" where we must each be responsible before God. As we apply God-ordained wisdom, no matter what we read, whether Lewis, Calvin or Morecraft, we are each responsible as a Christian reader to "rightly divide the word of truth." You must always wear the spectacles of Biblical discernment.

We live *coram Deo* before the face of God and are responsible before Him for everything we do--every minute of time, every thought and every idle word. I believe I can read an imperfect book or story and separate the wheat from the chaff. I have a well-honed blade from years of practice. The problem with this, however, especially for the young or immature reader, is that the written word can be even more seductive than the silver screen. Let the reader beware!

General categories of books you should scratch off your reading list:

- Soupy, mush-filled romances that claim to be Christian
- Poorly-written books, stories or any sloppily-written works that claim to be Christian
- Books full of images or language that portray sinful behavior as good or glorifies evil
- Articles, essays, stories or other writings that present inaccuracies in the depiction of characters or events if actual historical events are involved
- Slanderous stories, the author weaves his opinions about a person, movement, group or nation into a story, article or essay in such a way that the reader forms negative opinions about them which may be undeserved

I realize some books I recommend, including my "list-maker books," may not match your personal criteria. I hope we can meet on comfortable "middle ground" and decide how to apply the basic Biblical principles for ourselves. I have attempted to list books with basic Christian principles behind or underlying them even if they are not written for the purpose of stating Christian truth. We will find some writers who are so profoundly influenced by the Bible's teachings that their literary works promote or at least exhibit the influence of Christianity whether the writer was a proponent of Christianity or not.

Thank you for understanding my dilemma. As with all things in this fallen world, there are no perfect books since all are written by sinful men and women, therefore, there can be no flawless lists of book recommendations. I hope you will strive to develop a Christian '"grid" based on a solid foundation of Biblical principles through which you sift and sort all that you read and write.

As you may guess, neither the categories nor the books listed in them are intended to be comprehensive. So many books to recommend, so little time!

Books about Words and Language

The Miracle of Language, by professor, writer and humorist, Richard Lederer traces the roots of our language through many twists and turns from its beginnings down to current use and abuse.

Anguished English and other titles, by Richard Lederer. I was first introduced to the writings of this college professor turned author through selections from his book of collected errors from student papers and other language mishaps. It left me nearly suffocating from continuous laughter.

Word Power Made Easy, by Norman Lewis, first published the year I was born (look it up!), encourages etymology studies and is the book that persuaded me to include an extensive vocabulary section to this coursework. Although there are a few examples I ran across that I wish were not in the book, in general, the value of his approach to expansion of your vocabulary and word usage is well worth skipping over that which may not measure up to our beliefs.

Words at Play, by Willard R. Espy

Complete Word Book, by Mary De Vries

An American Dictionary of the English Language, by Noah Webster

Roget's Thesaurus

Disclaimer: Even though the two books listed below make presumptuous claims of having a corner on the knowledge market, they actually can be valuable tools for setting standards. As usual, however, Christian reader, sift and sort.

100 Words Every High School Graduate Should Know, by the publishers of the American Heritage Dictionary (I used this book in our second webinar but substituted a few words and added explanations to several.)

The Dictionary of Cultural Literacy: What Every American Needs to Know, by E. D. Hirsch, Joseph F. Kett and James Trefill. The stated purpose of this book is to tag the "common knowledge or collective memory" of Americans, p. ix in the introduction. Again, as you read, watch for Biblically incorrect statements; however, I have found this book a valuable resource for various writing projects and just for entertainment. Of course, I read dictionaries, manuals about grammar, punctuation and encyclopedias for pleasure, so I may not have the same standards as others in this category.

Books on Writing Well

Here are some books I recommend for tightening the girth on the grammar saddle so you won't fall off when you're writing:

Writing to God's Glory: A Comprehensive Creative Writing Course from Crayon to Quill, by Jill Bond. This excellent creative writing resource is replete with instructions, examples and assignments that provide ample practice for young writers from a Biblical worldview and it's lots of fun.

Painless Grammar, by Rebecca Elliott, is one of the best "user-friendly" grammar books around. I love its updated approach.

On Writing Well, the Classic Guide to Writing Nonfiction, by William Zinsser, is easy to read and practical.

Elements of Style, by Strunk and White is the "classic" book on developing a writing style, bar none.

The Only Grammar Book You'll Ever Need, by Susan Thurman, is an excellent resource for writing every type of paper, plus valuable appendices in the back entitled "1001 Frequently Misspelled Words," "Suggested Substitutes for Wordy Phrases," and "Helpful Grammar and Writing Web Sites."

Any Child Can Write, by Harvey S. Wiener

Woe is I, by Patricia O'Conner

The Grammar Devotional, by Mignon Fogarty

It Was the Best of Sentences, It Was the Worst of Sentences, by June Casagrande

Smart's Handbook of Effective Writing, by Walter K. Smart and Daniel R. Lang (first copyright, 1922)

100 Ways to Improve Your Writing, by Gary Provost

Where to start when recommending great literature! That's a challenge well-met by Vision Forum. Of course, you may have other resources, but if you want to check out their offerings, visit their web site.

Books Based on History, Historical Fiction

Historical fiction is my favorite genre. When the author is skillful, his story can transport you to places along the timeline of history where you can witness and vicariously experience God's providential hand at work in the events and lives of men, women and nations. Each title below can be found on the Vision Forum web site.

The Dragon and the Raven and other titles, by G. A. Henty. G. A. Henty's books are trustworthy accounts of history told through fiction.

The Coral Island and other titles, by R. M. Ballantyne.

The Betrayal and other titles, by Douglas Bond.

One modern writer well worth the read is Douglas Bond. His book about John Calvin provides insights into the enormity of the struggles experienced by the Reformers and will instill in your heart a new sense of gratitude for them. Told from the perspective of a sworn lifelong enemy of John Calvin, this fast-paced biographical novel is a tale of envy that escalates to violent intrigue and shameless betrayal.

Poetry Books and Books on Writing Poetry

The Roar on the Other Side, by Suzanne Rhodes. If you are interested in poetry writing, Suzanne Rhodes' book is one of the best around.

Listen to the Green and other titles, by Luci Shaw. Luci Shaw's poetic gift is rare indeed. She discovers metaphors and similes everywhere and distills poetry from them. I love Luci! I really enjoy her earlier works but all are intriguing as she finds "just the right word" or phrase to express the inexpressible. She writes primarily in blank or unrhymed verse.

Verses of Virtue, edited by Beall Phillips. I find myself grazing through this delicious book many times a day for encouragement, comfort and inspiration. Buy this for yourself and as gifts for those women and girls you love.

Poems for Patriarchs, edited by Douglas W. Phillips. This volume contains some of my favorite poems, those read to me by my grandfather, aunt and mother as I was growing up. Many are favorites for memorization as well. Doug Phillips has given us a treasure with this collection of time-honored classics.

The Pilgrim's Progress by John Bunyan is a book beloved, not only by my seven-year old granddaughter Anita, but for many generations of Christians. Written by a Puritan preacher who was incarcerated for his unyielding beliefs, the tale of Christian's journey through the hazards and blessings of life until he reaches glory, will warn, amaze and delight readers of any age. Vision Forum's heirloom edition will be loved and passed down through many of your generations:

> "Next to the Bible, *The Pilgrim's Progress* is the most widely distributed and popular book ever published. No Christian's education is complete without a thorough acquaintance with Bunyan's life-changing allegory. The simplicity, brilliance, and beauty of this timeless story have transformed untold lives. Now, *The Pilgrim's Progress* is available in an exquisite family heirloom edition, reprinted in its entirety from a 125-year-old historical compilation. This classic tome has been painstakingly reproduced with the same look and beautiful feel of the original and includes such rare treasures as Bunyan's memoirs, his last sermon, *The Holy War*, and over a dozen beautifully detailed artistic etchings. A massive, oversized, hardback edition, this volume contains the following works: *The Pilgrim's Progress*, *The Holy War*, *Grace Abounding to the Chief of Sinners*, *The Imprisonment and Release of John Bunyan*, *Bunyan's Dying Sayings*, *Christian Behaviour*, *The Barren Fig-Tree*, *Bunyan's Last Sermon*, and *The Water of Life*."

Theology

Authentic Christianity: Commentaries on the Westminster Larger Catechism, and other titles by Joseph C. Morecraft, III. Did you think I wouldn't recommend my husband's commentaries? (His lectures are widely available at Vision Forum as well as a wide selection at www.sermonaudio.com). These five commentaries are available both from American Vision or Vision Forum. They are the product of over 20 years of work as the author preached through the Westminster Larger Catechism. These volumes are very practical and scholarly at once and are useful for a thorough and precise understanding of Scripture as only this expanded catechism gives us.

The Institutes of the Christian Religion, and other titles by John Calvin

The Institutes of Biblical Law and other titles by R. J. Rushdoony, perhaps the most important theologian of our times.

The Sovereignty of God, by A. W. Pink. "Who is regulating affairs on this earth today—God or the devil?"

By This Standard, by Greg Bahnsen. Does God's law apply today?

Knowing God, by J. I. Packer

The Reformed Faith, by Robert Shaw (a commentary on the Westminster Confession of Faith)

The Westminster Shorter Catechism: for Study Classes, by G. I. Williamson—great for children

Spiritual Depression, its Causes and Cures, by D. Martyn Lloyd-Jones

A Crook in the Lot, the Sovereignty and Wisdom of God, by Puritan Thomas Boston

Matthew Henry's Commentary on the Bible, by Matthew Henry

Suggested Reading for Collections of Letters and Journals

Diary of a Southern Refugee During the War, by Judith B. McGuire, Sprinkle Publications

The Children of Pride: Selected letters of the family of the Rev. Dr. Charles Colcock Jones from the years 1860-1868; A New, Abridged Edition [Abridged], by Robert Manson Myers, Vail-Ballou Press, Binghamton, NY, 1978.

Best of Covered Wagon Women, Vol.s 1 & 2, edited by Kenneth L. Holmes, University of Oklahoma Press: Norman, OK, 2008.

Familiar Letters of John Adams and His Wife Abigail Adams, During the Revolution, by Charles Francis Adams, Hurd and Houghton, Cambridge: The Riverside Press, 1876.

Of Plymouth Plantation, by William Bradford,

The Journals of Captain Cook, by James Cook

The Journals of Lewis and Clark, by William Clark

The Diary of Kenneth MacCrae, by Kenneth MacCrae (a Scottish preacher at the turn of the 20th century)

The Diary of John Evelyn, by John Evelyn (a Puritan businessman)

The Letterbook of Eliza Lucas Pinckney (selected portions available from Vision Forum as an audio book)

History

The History of the Reformation and other titles, by J.H. Merle d'Aubigné

The Secret Six and other titles, by Otto Scott

For You They Signed, by Marilyn Boyer, the stories of the signers of the Declaration of Independence

Providential Battles, by Christian historian William Potter. With his usual acuity and verve, historian Bill Potter regales us with detailed analyses of twenty of the greatest battles in the history of the world that altered history.

The History of the Reformation, by Joe Morecraft, III. Fifty-five audio lectures on the Reformation.

Ideas Have Consequences, by Joe Morecraft, III. Four lectures on the colonization of America.

Audio-Books and More

I love dramatic readings! Next to the Bible, these classics are among those that have had the most impact on the Christian faith. Here in one collection, five classics, each in an easy-to-follow style with an introduction that provides the historical backdrop. The stories are vividly and compellingly narrated by master storyteller Max McLean. Listen to the most dramatic conversion to Christ since Paul's on the road to Damascus, as St. Augustine gives his testimony. Join Martin Luther as he is called to defend his writings against the established church. Hear Jonathan Edwards deliver the most famous sermon ever preached on American soil "Sinners in the Hands of an Angry God," and George Whitefield as he preaches during the Great Awakening. Finally, enjoy Bunyan's beautiful and moving abridged allegory of *The Pilgrim's Progress*. Listen and experience the power of these classics:

Elsie Dinsmore, by Martha Finley, audio book edition available from Vision Forum:

There are many other audio books available at the Vision Forum web site. Another favorite is by my friend Jennie Chancey, *Jennie B. and the Pilot*.

And finally, my favorite preacher and personal prophet, my husband Joe Morecraft, provides some free downloadable history lectures at www.sermonaudio.com:

The History of the Reformation, by Joe Morecraft, III. Fifty-five audio lectures on the Reformation.

Ideas Have Consequences, by Joe Morecraft, III. Four lectures on the colonization of America.

General Category: Inspiration

When I need encouragement as a woman fighting against the world's evil culture and the compromise of God's standards found even within many churches and Christians today, I pull out books that tell of the strong faith and actions of women and men of Reformation times.

Famous Women of the Reformed Church will inspire you and make you brave.

Stepping Heavenward should be read at least once a year by Christian women. So much can be gleaned from this wonderful book—comfort in sorrow, dealing with pride, the rewards of relying on God—a "must-have" for every woman's library.

Biography

Visit the Vision Forum web site to find many great biographies available. Some of my favorites include:

The Adventures of Missionary Heroism, by John Lambert

Missionary Patriarch, the True Story of John G. Paton, Evangelist for Jesus Christ Among the South Sea Cannibals, by John G. Paton

The Scots Worthies, by John Howie

Reformation Heroes, by Diana Kleyn and Joel Beeke

Alone, Yet Not Alone, by Tracy Leininger

Beloved Bride: The Letters of Stonewall Jackson to His Wife, by Bill Potter

John Calvin, Man of the Millennium, by Phillip Vellmer, edited by Wesley Strackbein

Children's Books

Here's my theory and I'm sticking to it: the family that reads books together, aloud, as a part of their weekly fellowship, will always be "on the same page." My parents, grandparents and aunt read to us aloud often as a child and still love the sound of my mother's voice reading some favorite passage from a book, old or new. I am comforted and still inspired by the memory of my grandparents' voices as they read or quoted favorite stories, poems and passages from the Bible aloud. Even now, visits home are never complete without my dear Papa's voice reading Scripture or Spurgeon's *Morning and Evening* devotional to the gathered family.

    Nothing makes me happier today than reading some of my favorite books and theirs to my grandchildren. Not just any book will do. I try to read stories to my grandchildren that are beautifully written with an underlying Biblical theme, pleasing to the eye and ears. I love beautifully illustrated books for children, too. Books will influence us much like jumping into a strong stream that leads to an ocean: we will be carried along in one direction or another. Make sure you are aware of the currents as you read. Choose the "ocean" towards which you want your children aimed.

APPENDIX D: RECOMMENDED READING LISTS & MORE

Reading aloud is one of life's pleasures, bringing blessings to both the reader and the recipient. Reading alone is a treasured blessing like no other. Books can take you to places you may never visit except in your mind--you can travel back in history or into the future, visit desert islands, medieval castles or lush forests in the Amazon valley or escape into hidden valleys in the Alps or the Appalachian Mountains. Well-written books take the reader wherever the skillful author weaves his path. And as you broaden your vocabulary and hone your writing skills, look for opportunities to grow spiritually, socially and mentally as the Lord works noble thoughts and spiritual truths into your heart and mind through your reading.

My husband likes to say, "Those who read lead." If you want to be a leader, a well-grounded father in the home and mother to your children, you must be a reader. We are called as Christians, not only to follow our great Leader, the Lord Jesus, but to imitate Him in all our choices and even our preferences. Make wise choices in your reading preferences. Here are some lists of books I like and some that I love. This list is far from complete. I have many other recommendations.

Honey for a Child's Heart by Gladys Hunt. This was the first book I used to help in book selections when my children were small. Now in its fourth edition, you will find it spiritually uplifting as well as informative. I still have the first edition and cannot tell you about the more recent ones--you are on your own here.

The Book Tree, by Elizabeth McCallum and her daughter Jane Scott, should be in every Christian home. Both of these books set out a Christian philosophy for choosing books as well as commentary on each selection.

Pre-School (Age 5 and Under)

Winnie the Pooh and related titles, by A. A. Milne

Goodnight Moon, by Margaret Wise Brown

The Very Hungry Caterpillar, by Eric Carle

Blueberries for Sal, and other titles by Robert McCloskey

The Child's Story Bible, by Catherine F. Vos

Guess How Much I Love You, by Sam McBratney

All the Places to Love, by Patricia MacLachlan

Little Bear, and other titles by Else H. Minarik

Owl Moon, by Jane Yolen

The Little Engine That Could, by Watty Piper

Peter and the Wolf (the musical edition), by Sergei Prokofiev

The Tale of Peter Rabbit and other titles, by Beatrix Potter

Curious George and other titles, by Hans Rey

A Child's Garden of Verses and other titles, by Robert Louis Stevenson

The Lord is My Shepherd and other titles, by illustrator Tasha Tudor

Elementary Fiction (Ages 6-12)

Aesop's Fables, by Aesop

Treasury of Fairy Tales, by Hans Christian Anderson

The Mitten and other titles, by Jan Brett

Caddie Woodlawn, by Carol Ryrie Brink

The Pied Piper of Hamelin and other titles, by Robert Browning

Riding the Pony Express, by Clyde Robert Bulla

The Incredible Journey, by Shelia Burnford

The Courage of Sarah Noble and other titles, by Alice Dalgliesh

Hans Brinker and the Silver Skates, by Mary Maples Dodge

William Tell, by Margaret Early

The Matchlock Gun, by Walter D. Edmonds

Old Yeller, by Fred Gipson

Tanglewood Tales and select other titles, by Nathaniel Hawthorne

Saint George and the Dragon, by Margaret Hodges

Huguenot Garden and other titles, by Douglas M. Jones, III

Frog and Toad and other titles, by Arnold Lobel

Hiawatha and other titles, by Henry Wadsworth Longfellow

The Lost Princess; At the Back of the North Wind and other titles, by George MacDonald

Iron Scouts of the Confederacy, by Lee McGiffin

Sarah, Plain and Tall, by Patricia MacLachlan

Anne of Green Gables and other titles, by L. M. Montgomery

The Railway Children and other titles, by E. Nesbit

Annie Henry and the Redcoats and other titles, by Susan Olasky

Two Little Confederates and select other titles, by Thomas Nelson Page

Treasures in the Snow, by Patricia St. John

Five Little Peppers and How They Grew and other titles, by Margaret Sidney

The Bronze Bow and other titles, by Elizabeth Speare

Heidi, by Johanna Spyri

Little House on the Prairie and other titles, by Laura Ingalls Wilder

Middle School Fiction (Ages 12+)

Little Women and other titles, by Louisa May Alcott

Coral Island and other titles, by R. M. Ballantyne

The Pilgrim's Progress, by John Bunyan

The Canterbury Tales, by Geoffrey Chaucer, adapted by Barbara Cohen

The Moonstone, by Wilkie Collins

Great Expectations and other titles, by Charles Dickens

The Adventures of Robinson Crusoe and other titles, by Daniel Defoe

The Memoirs of Sherlock Holmes, by Sir Arthur Conan Doyle

The Count of Monte Cristo and other titles, by Alexandre Dumas

Johnny Tremain, by Esther Forbes

Lieutenant Hornblower and other titles, by C. S. Forester

The Gift of the Magi and other titles, by O. Henry

The Dragon and the Raven and other titles, by G. A. Henty

All Things Bright and Beautiful and other titles, by James Herriott

Hind's Feet on High Places, by Hannah Hurnard

Tales from Shakespeare, by Charles and Mary Lamb

Brothers of the Sled, by John Leeper

The Scarlet Pimpernel, by Baroness Emmuska Orczy

The Girl of the Limberlost; *Freckles* and other titles, by Gene Stratton Porter

A White Bird Flying; *A Lantern in Her Hand* and other titles, by Bess Streeter Aldrich

Men of Iron and other titles, by Howard Pyle

Light in the Forest, by Conrad Richter

Beowulf the Warrior and other titles, by Ian Serraillier, translator

Kidnapped and other titles, by Robert Louis Stevenson

Betty Zane and other titles, by Zane Grey

Around the World in Eighty Days and other titles, by Jules Verne

Augustine Comes to Kent and other titles, by Barbara Willard

The Horn of Roland and other titles, by Jay Williams

The Swiss Family Robinson, by Johann R. Wyss

Elementary and Middle School Biography (Ages 12+)

Augustine, the Farmer's Boy of Tagaste, by P. de Zeeuw

The Talking Wire: The Story of Alexander Graham Bell, by O. J. Stevenson

Daniel Boone, by James Daugherty

Carry on, Mr. Bowditch, by Jean Lee Latham

Alone, Yet Not Alone, by Tracy Leininger

The Columbus Story, by Alice Dalgliesh

A Confederate Trilogy, by Mary L. Williamson

Robert Fulton, Boy Crasftsman and other titles, by Marguerite Henry

George Fredric Handel, Composer of Messiah, by Charles Ludwig

Stonewall, by Jean Fritz

Johannes Kepler: Giant of Science, by John Judson Tiner

Robert E. Lee: Christian General and Gentleman, by Roddy Lee

Eric Liddell, by Catherine Swift

Queen of the Reformation, Katherine Luther, by Charles Ludwig

The Light in the Darkness, edited by James and Stacy McDonald

Matthew Wheelock's Wall, by Frances Ward Weller. Most of the books I've listed above are for high school age and above. But I love some children's books as much as those targeted for adults. The simplicity of style is refreshing and since short words are used generally, these books make good models for aspiring writers. One such book with a deep and abiding message: that of building for future generations is *Matthew Wheelock's Wall*, written by Frances Ward Weller and illustrated beautifully by Ted Lewin.

Christian Romance
(That is, tales of adventure with love stories woven into them.)

To Have and To Hold and other titles, by Mary Johnston

Ivanhoe and other titles, by Sir Walter Scott

The Princess Adelina, by Julie Sutter

There are many more books I'd like to suggest in this category. Some overlap into other categories such as biography or age-sensitive categories; but, alas, time and space bring me to a screeching close. Write me at **mrs.morecraft@gmail.com** for further recommendations or to give me your suggestions.

I hope I've given you plenty of ideas for reading materials to delight and inspire you as you sit by the fireside or snuggle under a cozy quilt or with a cool summer sip by the pool. I pray that finding and reading good books will be an adventure that will never end!

Happy Reading!
Mrs. Morecraft

APPENDIX E
Vocabulary Lists

"In the beginning was the Word and the Word was with God and the Word was God." —John 1:1

God loves words. His Son is called "The Word," or the best expression of Who God is in the flesh: "And the Word became flesh and dwelt among us." Because God loves words, we should love them, too.

Writing well involves several elements which, like a good recipe, must be carefully planned, revised and then consumed with delight. Generally speaking, the most appetizing and satisfying dishes are prepared with fresh ingredients, the right blend of contrasting flavors, textures and colors. Whenever possible, a dish should be tasted occasionally during preparation to determine whether the final result will be palate-pleasing or if it needs "editing." No reputable chef would dream of throwing a dish together without a well thought-out plan and the proper equipment and ingredients.

In much the same way, a serious writer must go through several steps before he ultimately presents his writing project for the scrutiny of discerning readers. We will discuss the particulars of the process in other places; but the one that we are concerned with at this juncture is word choice. In the kitchen, it's really important to know the difference between paprika and cayenne pepper. Although the two spices are nearly identical in color and texture, the difference in flavor and heat is rather remarkable, to put it mildly.

Similarly, when a writer searches for a word that will best express what he is attempting to say, finding the exact word is critically important. The thesaurus and dictionary are two invaluable tools in this process. But another facet of honing your word-searching skills is word-gathering, gleaning words from literally every source where they are to be found–from books, sermons, lectures, letters, magazine articles, ad campaigns, jar labels, seed catalogs, speeches, plays, movies, children at play, even lectures on how to write: enter stage left, Mrs. Morecraft.

I am making your job a bit easier here. I plan to go through my lectures and pull out a list of words I think you should know. You may already know the general definition of most of them. Bravo! But, do you know the etymology, or how the word was "born," its history? Do you know its synonyms and antonyms? Its common uses?

In this appendix you will find words I think you should study and "own." I want you to do three things with them:

1. First, look up the standard definition of each word in a reliable dictionary. I strongly recommend Noah Webster's 1828 Dictionary sold by Vision Forum. Many of the definitions are highly Biblical in content. Of course, most of us have good dictionary resources installed in our computers, so this is an easy option.

2. Second, memorize the spelling and pronunciation of the word.

3. Third, write two sentences using the word or its relatives in slightly different ways where it would be helpful. Be sure to remember the difference in denotation and connotation here.

4. Fourth, look at the etymology, or derivation, of the word and begin to associate its roots with other words springing from the same roots. This will greatly increase your ability to instantly figure out unfamiliar words and increase your reading vocabulary exponentially. If you need to do so, go back over those sections of our lectures that explain how to use etymology to increase your word power.

5. Fifth, list some of the synonyms and then a few antonyms of the word.

You may organize your vocabulary list in several different ways. In one of the first classes I suggested that you create lists of strong verbs and interesting nouns. That's one way–listing words as parts of speech. However, there are other ways that may be more useful. As you uncover the roots of words, you could begin a "word family" set of lists, adding words in the same grouping that grew out of the same roots.

Of course, you can also simply alphabetize the words or just list them in no particular order. This is completely your decision–make a list that works for you. The goal is that you develop an expanded working vocabulary, (or words that you actually incorporate into your conversation and writing), and an even larger reading vocabulary.

Another suggestion is to have lists of common words, usually short, strong words at hand. List them as nouns and verbs or in whatever way makes sense to you. Most of the words you use in writing should be easily recognizable by your intended audience and, in general, the short words in English are stronger than longer ones. It's just a thought. Have fun! You may become a logophile like me! (Look it up!)

Example of vocabulary exercises:

1. **Mesmerize:** (a transitive verb) to fascinate or absorb all of someone's attention.
"The speaker mesmerized the audience with his dramatic voice."
"The baby seemed mesmerized by the cat's antics."

   Mesmerizer: (a noun) one who has the ability to mesmerize. Other forms of this word: mesmerization, n.; mesmerizingly, adv.

   Synonyms: hypnotize, captivate, enthrall, absorb, entrance, spellbind, rivet, charm, fascinate, excite, thrill

   Antonym: bore

   Word History: (or etymology)

   Mesmerize: Date of Origin, 19th c.

"Franz Anton Mesmer (1734–1815) was an Austrian doctor whose experiments with what he called 'animal magnetism', by which he induced a trance-like state in his subjects, are considered to be the forerunner of modern hypnotism (formerly called mesmerism (19th c.)). The broader sense of mesmerize, 'enthral', dates from the early 20th century."

www.word-origins.com/definition/mesmerize.html

Vocabulary Lists
(Suggested: Look-Up 10 a Day)

1. cultivate
2. ottoman
3. exposition
4. wield
5. magnify
6. delve
7. narrative
8. weigh
9. burden
10. scope
11. worth
12. decipher
13. illiterate
14. fluent
15. immortal
16. bard
17. vent
18. insistent
19. convey
20. hone
21. tribute
22. verse
23. pithy
24. blight
25. hollow
26. clump
27. clog
28. distill
29. prune
30. impact
31. earthy
32. imagery
33. canker
34. flicker
35. mindset
36. worldview
37. conscience
38. fragrant
39. reside
40. ordain
41. delete
42. tweak
43. clarify
44. conglomeration
45. gene
46. similar
47. unique
48. velum
49. illuminate
50. script
51. relevant
52. accustom
53. mention
54. sonata
55. pesky
56. expand
57. original
58. boggle
59. grid
60. conformity
61. edify
62. sanctification
63. coram Deo
64. valid
65. gird
66. arch
67. convince
68. antithesis
69. oblige

APPENDIX E: VOCABULARY LISTS

70. opine
71. destination
72. develop
73. definite
74. metaphor
75. simile
76. figurative
77. analyze
78. entry
79. portion
80. consideration
81. extol
82. conversion
83. repentant
84. condone
85. culture
86. fantasy
87. embark
88. fascination
89. redeem
90. meager
91. sphere
92. tackle
93. modicum
94. glare
95. laser
96. intentional
97. factor
98. transition
99. resource
100. modifier
101. represent
102. framework
103. synonym
104. antonym
105. homonym
106. pseudonym
107. advent
108. dowry
109. negotiate
110. degeneration
111. resource
112. precise
113. convenience
114. underpin
115. undergird
116. overarch
117. element
118. grace
119. industrious
120. whimsical
121. musings
122. elocution
123. accessible
124. designate
125. accurate
126. incorporate
127. jog
128. construct
129. renown
130. imitate
131. thrill
132. foundation
133. firm
134. access
135. technical
136. challenge
137. frustration
138. key
139. question
140. participate
141. visual
142. solidify
143. pertain
144. abbreviate
145. code
146. pertain
147. proofread

148. trendy
149. plunge
150. section
151. tackle
152. slash
153. sidebar
154. capacity
155. weighty
156. tacky
157. garment
158. particular
159. accessories
160. elegance
161. lookout
162. ransom
163. proposal
164. ancient
165. tutorial
166. fortune
167. snoop
168. frame
169. discipline
170. technique
171. tense
172. form
173. progressive

174. tartlet
175. forte
176. tote
177. ebb
178. flow
179. acknowledge
180. situation
181. irregular
182. situation
183. patch
184. complicate
185. variation
186. contradict
187. repetitive
188. consistent
189. cramp
190. requirement
191. constraint
192. principle
193. vignette
194. accurate
195. develop
196. spontaneous
197. forethought
198. genre
199. fertile

200. jot
201. crowd
202. frequent
203. seminar
204. tutelage
205. imagery
206. mortify
207. voluminous
208. chug
209. pseudo
210. keeper
211. amidst
212. eventuate
213. ignite
214. slightly
215. inflexible
216. disturb
217. appropriate
218. principle
219. desert
220. benefit
221. consider
222. convenience
223. fame
224. rude
225. technical

APPENDIX E: VOCABULARY LISTS

226. marbles
227. clomp
228. convey
229. faculties
230. gifted
231. process
232. mystery
233. pathway
234. anomalous
235. unsolicited
236. lees
237. scudding
238. drifts
239. vex
240. dim
241. peers
242. gleams
243. margin
244. unburnished
245. chaos
246. ample
247. focus
248. spring
249. harbinger
250. glimmer
251. filter

252. bin
253. audio
254. unique
255. indebted
256. furious
257. loom
258. spool
259. craft
260. grandiose
261. glut
262. ingenious
263. quip
264. vitriolic
265. sturdy
266. utilize
267. advantage
268. trap
269. trade
270. transform
271. soar
272. sonnet
273. self-expression
274. release
275. captive
276. slimy
277. slug

278. slink
279. heritage
280. symbolism
281. scatter
282. briary
283. branch
284. gnarly
285. transplant
286. patch
287. borne
288. remembrance
289. quench
290. toil
291. generations
292. heeling in
293. sod
294. graces
295. trace
296. pattern
297. nothingness
298. vast
299. overwhelm
300. ex nihilo
301. forefront
302. awe
303. comprehend

304. manifest
305. definitive
306. unfathomable
307. incomprehensible
308. depth
309. breadth
310. extent
311. unspeakable
312. shadow
313. fester
314. balm
315. intimate
316. certainty
317. vital
318. assist
319. strive
320. employ
321. expand
322. rational
323. sequence
324. further
325. intently
326. involve
327. flight
328. symbolism
329. impel

330. complex
331. patterns
332. succinct
333. pithy
334. express
335. convey
336. elements
337. conveyance
338. depiction
339. elevate
340. reminiscent
341. facet
342. scope
343. dimension
344. variety
345. replete
346. garment
347. swaddling
348. decree
349. hitherto
350. further
351. stay
352. wither
353. prosper
354. chaff
355. sensory

356. palpable
357. processes
358. craft
359. employ
360. mead
361. vale
362. stab
363. ingenious
364. spontaneous
365. overflow
366. recollect
367. tranquility
368. lyrical
369. ballad
370. journey
371. excerpt
372. exact
373. minute
374. visual
375. auditory
376. sensory
377. real-life
378. transitional
379. snag
380. visualize
381. prop

APPENDIX E: VOCABULARY LISTS

382. zenith
383. drop
384. faint
385. clink
386. recount
387. vivid
388. dipper
389. flavor
390. seal
391. plant
392. sprinkle
393. rapturous
394. bed down
395. slumber
396. consciousness
397. association
398. significance
399. inclination
400. evoke
401. nucleus
402. cluster
403. diagram
404. central
405. reflection
406. emanate
407. concrete
408. abstract
409. generalize
410. response
411. personification
412. apostrophe
413. hyperbole
414. understatement
415. device
416. doomed
417. narrator
418. inanimate
419. abstraction
420. dissolve
421. intense
422. fitted
423. inexpressible
424. ploy
425. employ
426. incorporate
427. advantage
428. comparison
429. subsume
430. subsistence
431. elevate
432. drawn
433. tactile
434. allusion
435. apt
436. discretion
437. weathered
438. association
439. envision
440. surge
441. rasp
442. preposition
443. noun
444. pronoun
445. verb
446. disapprove
447. dialogue
448. structure
449. construction
450. variation
451. blunder
452. memorialize
453. gallant
454. whirlwind
455. galaxy
456. poignant
457. quest
458. formation
459. elaboration

460. conflict
461. energize
462. subversion
463. sentiment
464. legitimate
465. self-expression
466. convey
467. convictions
468. grasp
469. convict
470. ghetto
471. sustenance
472. plunge
473. wrung-out
474. objective
475. focus
476. compelling
477. alternative
478. status quo
479. devices
480. protocol
481. mastery
482. penchant
483. captivating
484. admonition
485. quarter
486. slay
487. emasculate
488. helpmeet
489. portion
490. essay
491. futile
492. feminism
493. reclaim
494. superior
495. keenly
496. striking
497. groupings
498. vast
499. ample
500. obsessive
501. supple
502. root (v.)
503. exclusive
504. lexicon
505. fragrant
506. nourishing
507. official
508. converse
509. disposal
510. mingled
511. distinctive
512. tier
513. Anglo-Saxon
514. classical
515. approximate
516. illustrate
517. interrogate
518. defunct
519. conclude
520. trepidation
521. assist
522. ascend
523. emaciated
524. livelier
525. tongue
526. directness
527. brevity
528. plainness
529. production
530. statistic
531. ongoing
532. lemata (Latin)
533. dreary
534. accommodation
535. aerial
536. amazement
537. apostrophe

APPENDIX E: VOCABULARY LISTS

538. assassination
539. auspicious
540. baseless
541. castigate
542. clangor
543. dexterous
544. dwindle
545. fitful
546. frugal
547. impartial
548. lapse
549. multitudinous
550. obscene
551. pedant
552. perusal
553. pious
554. radiance
555. sanctimonious
556. seamy
557. sportive
558. submerge
559. compound
560. barefaced
561. civil-tongued
562. cold comfort
563. eyesore
564. fancy free
565. foregone conclusion
566. foul play
567. green-eyed
568. heartsick
569. high time
570. hotblooded
571. itching palm
572. lackluster
573. laughing-stock
574. leapfrog
575. lie low
576. long-hair
577. ministering angel
578. pitched battle
579. primrose path
580. short shrift
581. snow-white
582. stony-hearted
583. tongue-tied
584. towering passion
585. yeoman's service
586. cliché
587. reaction
588. memorable
589. proverbial
590. brevity
591. the rub
592. method in madness
593. apparel
594. borrower
595. lender
596. frailty
597. protest
598. epithet
599. pun
600. intrigue
601. moorings
602. revamp
603. enrich
604. vessel
605. maneuver
606. sea-worthy
607. exotic
608. venue
609. hold
610. prefabricated
611. inherent
612. abound
613. resourceful

614. inform
615. particulars
616. compact
617. constraint
618. competence
619. aspire
620. essay
621. attest
622. word-picture
623. preference
624. mentor
625. definite
626. compact
627. contrived
628. trite
629. proven
630. plainness
631. simplicity
632. orderliness
633. sincerity
634. laborious
635. cultivate
636. proficient
637. emerge
638. barrier
639. principal
640. composition
641. imitate
642. interact
643. inferior
644. echo
645. guidelines
646. emphasize
647. specific
648. observe
649. literary
650. inaccuracy
651. color
652. lurk
653. enrich
654. extensive
655. range
656. palette
657. heir
658. miracle
659. glean
660. impetus
661. enlarge
662. mastery
663. primary
664. source
665. energy
666. charge
667. valuable
668. assistant
669. dullness
670. define
671. specific
672. dependent
673. inactive
674. sharpen
675. stare
676. gaze
677. peer
678. peek
679. gawk
680. flip
681. hurl
682. active voice
683. passive voice
684. emphasis
685. density
686. hoist
687. barbarity
688. savagery
689. brutality
690. connotation
691. denotation

APPENDIX E: VOCABULARY LISTS

692. gaslight
693. infuse
694. word picture
695. enhance
696. adorn
697. modify
698. adjective
699. adverb
700. awkward
701. gradation
702. branch
703. conjure
704. cajole
705. wheedle
706. blandish
707. coax
708. villain
709. awash
710. rascality
711. lexicographer
712. iniquity
713. obliquity
714. depravity
715. knavery
716. infamy
717. ruffian

718. riffraff
719. miscreant
720. malefactor
721. reprobate
722. rapscallion
723. hooligan
724. hoodlum
725. scamp
726. scapegoat
727. scoundrel
728. scalawag
729. foul
730. fiendish
731. devilish
732. diabolical
733. cross-reference
734. thicket
735. nudge
736. rummage
737. network
738. meter
739. alliteration
740. vital
741. stylist
742. cadence
743. sonority

744. relish
745. surmise
746. linger
747. plodding
748. gait
749. alter
750. punch
751. revision
752. transpose
753. voila!
754. envision
755. ornate
756. overblown
757. compensate
758. vigor
759. wordiness
760. ruthless
761. excess
762. overstatement
763. diminish
764. superlative
765. qualifier
766. leech
767. infest
768. alter
769. violate

770. uninhibited
771. spontaneity
772. provocation
773. ingenuity
774. patronizing
775. pretentious
776. reign
777. disclosure
778. clutter
779. annoy
780. attributive
781. explanatory
782. console
783. obscure
784. imposition
785. vital
786. handy
787. atrocious
788. felicitous
789. alarming
790. colloquialism
791. rigidity
792. split infinitive
793. deceptive
794. contrived
795. mire
796. syntax
797. misplaced
798. slipshod
799. neutrality
800. unwieldy
801. cumbersome
802. surefooted
803. fluent
804. expostulate
805. pompous
806. readership
807. self-explanatory
808. verbiage
809. jargon
810. slang
811. segment
812. momentarily
813. passé
814. sound bite
815. employ
816. breezy
817. catchy
818. innovator
819. extinction
820. scrawl
821. decode
822. enrichment
823. presupposition
824. creative
825. cozy
826. transforming
827. hardwood
828. spectacular
829. handiwork
830. cider
831. spice
832. dollop
833. consent
834. postpone
835. festival
836. honorable
837. bonus
838. feedback
839. devote
840. intend
841. moderation
842. accuracy
843. epistles
844. comprise
845. exile
846. recipients
847. colorful

848. rebuke
849. admonish
850. mentor
851. scrutinize
852. toss
853. search engine
854. access
855. networking
856. intact
857. besmirch
858. encompass
859. document
860. imaginative
861. incorporate
862. pleasurable
863. administrator
864. decade
865. relatively
866. rise (v.)
867. admiralty
868. subsequent
869. detailed
870. incident
871. beneficial
872. penmanship
873. spark

874. track
875. wit
876. pluck
877. sense
878. continuity
879. central
880. compartments
881. evident
882. selective
883. incidents
884. townspeople
885. providence
886. happenings
887. completion
888. convenience
889. depict
890. caption
891. blur
892. reaction
893. journal
894. portfolio
895. diligent
896. sequence
897. pronoun
898. reality
899. reflexive

900. relative
901. imply
902. antecedent
903. clause
904. phrase
905. scramble
906. substitute
907. previous
908. in-depth
909. capacity
910. system
911. categorize
912. application
913. enthusiasm
914. sideline
915. terminology
916. related
917. details
918. vague
919. standards
920. etiquette
921. salutation
922. primary
923. resource
924. frequent
925. engage

926. supervision	952. essential	978. posture
927. painstaking	953. epistolary	979. employ
928. gauge	954. inclination	980. discard
929. surname	955. affirmation	981. surname
930. recipient	956. perfidious	982. petition
931. collectible	957. superimpose	983. convey
932. details	958. three-dimensional	984. plainspoken
933. tag	959. potent	985. landmark
934. attachment	960. declaration	986. assumption
935. appropriate	961. evanescent	987. incorporate
936. generic	962. mingle	988. whimsical
937. convey	963. systematic	989. reclaim
938. laborious	964. legible	990. exchange
939. after-thought	965. calligraphy	991. appropriate
940. tantalize	966. feat	992. attest
941. sequence	967. illuminated	993. disastrous
942. draft	968. ornamental	994. admonition
943. given	969. manuscripts	995. attestation
944. cogent	970. illustrative	996. intrigue
945. ramble	971. embossed	997. cherish
946. communication	972. stark	998. outpouring
947. admittance	973. vogue	999. collage
948. outline	974. nib	1000. souvenir
949. intersperse	975. blotch	1001. haven
950. ease	976. smear	1002. carve
951. grace	977. aromatic	1003. niche

1004. chaos
1005. conclusion
1006. awareness
1007. hieroglyphic
1008. replenish
1009. frantic
1010. appeal
1011. lend
1012. headlong
1013. rush
1014. gasp
1015. illegible
1016. empathy
1017. anecdotes
1018. pad
1019. extraneous
1020. excess
1021. draft
1022. vivid
1023. perspective
1024. reflection
1025. chase
1026. chill
1027. hearth
1028. crackle
1029. flames

1030. epic
1031. storyboarding
1032. aspect
1033. adequately
1034. availability
1035. pitfall
1036. encounter
1037. plunge
1038. exemplify
1039. contender
1040. reference
1041. resource
1042. genuine
1043. esteem
1044. observation
1045. disregard
1046. rhetoric
1047. compensation
1048. merit
1049. attain
1050. violation
1051. all right
1052. aggravate
1053. shrill
1054. contraction
1055. exception

1056. appropriate
1057. among
1058. between
1059. humility
1060. redundant
1061. rear (v.)
1062. conjunction
1063. restrictive
1064. symmetry
1065. sing-song
1066. contrast
1067. recast
1068. monotony
1069. semi-colon
1070. period
1071. accomplishment
1072. succession
1073. precedent
1074. embed
1075. hierarchy
1076. fugue
1077. claim
1078. maintain
1079. perpetrate
1080. glutinous
1081. momentum

1082. tug
1083. fitfully
1084. activate
1085. start
1086. launch
1087. resign
1088. exclamation point
1089. enhance
1090. gaudy
1091. effective
1092. employ
1093. stalwart
1094. insistence
1095. resistance
1096. subsequently
1097. process
1098. shift
1099. primed
1100. switch
1101. abrupt
1102. summarize
1103. despite
1104. always
1105. knavish
1106. forethought
1107. chivalry
1108. compassion
1109. wordiness
1110. oriented
1111. previously
1112. meanwhile
1113. now
1114. today
1115. later
1116. time frame
1117. compression
1118. proximity
1119. dimension
1120. rummage
1121. artful
1122. dazzling
1123. illumine
1124. euphony
1125. cacophony
1126. onomatopoeia
1127. assonance
1128. consonance
1129. alliteration
1130. rhyme
1131. defining
1132. factor
1133. medieval
1134. guise
1135. gear
1136. mantle
1137. embellish
1138. Beowulf
1139. Sir Gawain
1140. unify
1141. enliven
1142. exact rhyme
1143. end rhyme
1144. internal rhyme
1145. farewell
1146. adieu
1147. rejoin
1148. frosty
1149. thaw
1150. blaze
1151. imaginings
1152. confidence
1153. patience
1154. await
1155. pinnacle
1156. apex
1157. ascent
1158. summit
1159. secret passage

APPENDIX E: VOCABULARY LISTS

1160. glider
1161. crunchy
1162. crinkled
1163. litter
1164. tufts
1165. hickory
1166. pit
1167. hull
1168. prospects
1169. mid-stream
1170. various
1171. gluten
1172. privilege
1173. launch
1174. field
1175. endeavor
1176. loose ends
1177. tied up
1178. tarp
1179. paraphrase
1180. sovereignty
1181. redeem
1182. accomplish
1183. reality
1184. incarnation
1185. trace
1186. history of redemption
1187. cataclysm
1188. occurrence
1189. tapestry
1190. exhibit
1191. underside
1192. tapestry
1193. intricate
1194. design
1195. challenge
1196. unsearchable
1197. provision
1198. resources
1199. expressive
1200. observations
1201. anticipation
1202. inhibit
1203. creative
1204. mediocre
1205. partial
1206. plethora
1207. gumption
1208. influence
1209. complexity
1210. user-friendly
1211. ethical
1212. morality
1213. wholesome
1214. eliminate
1215. blatant
1216. objectionable
1217. perspective
1218. avoid
1219. critical
1220. analysis
1221. discernment
1222. garner
1223. sensibility
1224. serviceable
1225. veteran
1226. accuracy
1227. depict
1228. submit
1229. adventurous
1230. format
1231. appreciative
1232. distinction
1233. sole
1234. quantity
1235. nuance
1236. quality

1237. discretion

1238. avenue

1239. mix-up

1240. steed

1241. rhetoric

1242. resolve

1243. eloquent

1244. forceful

1245. embody

1246. flow

1247. uphold

1248. fold

1249. flagrant

1250. soupy

1251. texture

1252. scramble

1253. tidings

1254. quandary

1255. loathsome

1256. shriek

1257. stumble

1258. quarter

1259. quash

1260. invention